Best Manchester Poets

Volume 2

Puppywolf

*To Charlie
with Love.*

Steve

(p. 124)

Puppywolf
Manchester
United Kingdom
Web: http://www.puppywolf.co.uk
Email: enquiries@puppywolf.co.uk
Twitter: @puppywolfpoetry

Published December 2011.

A catalogue record for this book is available from the British Library.

ISBN 978-0-9565819-3-8

*In memory of the Greenroom theatre
and with thanks to the wonderful
staff who worked there.*

Gone but not forgotten.

*We will not forget why it closed
when we go to the ballot box.*

Contents

Foreword

"This is Manchester. We do things differently here."
— Anthony Wilson

Manchester is the creative capital of the United Kingdom. That's a bold claim, for sure, but one we've earned over the last four decades, perhaps more. Manchester's always been a bit odd in this way – for as long as the place has existed it's been possible to find arty enclaves defying the suggestion that it's grim up north.

Modern Manchester seems to specialise in generating raw and unbridled talent. Whatever the case, the swagger and bravado associated with Manchester comes out through the poetry of its inhabitants, and can be found in this book.

Yet like the first volume of BoMP published in 2010, this second volume of all-new poetry is a mixed bag. Yes, it takes from the vibrant and unique live poetry scene but also includes established names who are quite literally more at home in the serenity of BBC Radio 4. Additionally, the book is a platform for several writers who've never been published before, and we are extremely proud of this in particular. This year we extended our reach to include participants on the creative writing courses at Manchester's universities – this being another area where Manchester leads the way.

As always, thanks go out not only to the poets who submitted work (those who were successful and those who weren't) but also to the editors, whose job it was to read through hundreds of poems and give them their full attention. This book really is a labour of love – love being something else you'll find above average amounts of in Manchester.

Keir Thomas, Puppywolf
December 2011, Manchester

The poems

Ursula Hurley

I Will Pick Flowers for You

The horror and the bronze safety pin, empty now.
Still fixed to a black lapel where once it held a white
      chrysanthemum,
foraged on the morning of the day from amongst tough old
      chard
and nasturtiums knocked sprawling by frost.
Small, wet and slug-bitten.
A token of defiance and pounds saved at the florist.

Later, we stood on the patio, applying red wine
and menthol cigarettes to the wound. The sky gathered rain
      to its bosom,
sought to enfold us. Water dripped from the chestnut tree,
dying assuredly yet outliving us all. We gathered conkers on
      the dark lawn.
Needing to hold life in our hands and keep it.

JONNY RODGERS

Sunday Best

We took the bus into town
and he dropped his change instantly.
I held his elbow as we got off,
him grinning his head around
the shades I'd insisted upon.

He rubbed a dog's ears down
for a full five minutes
while two nutters slapped
each other's teeth across the pavement.

He didn't pay for anything.

I had to steer his shoulders away
from the people he thought he knew.

After one o'clock his beard remained
flecked with broken pastry.
His eyes bulged to the pierced
button of a teenage stomach.

We sat at the back going home,
him tipping a sweating Evian bottle
back and forth in front of his eyes.
He wouldn't say how the family was getting on.

I walked him through the twisted shrubs
and watched him jangle the tea things
through the back window;
he was measuring sugar through the holes in his hands.

ROD RIESCO

Indoor Landscape

In the Cumbrian village café we sit under a giant mural,
painted apparently with house paint and a four-inch brush.
The artist has restricted herself to green and blue
and helpfully written "Catbells" to identify
the shapeless surging body of emerald gloss under
a sky that differs from the earth in colour,
but not in texture. She has expressed some
grand swirl of emotion, perhaps, or needed to cover
a certain square footage, above the pine tables.

Nothing resembles the hill where we have just walked,
with its bony spine, the russet and ginger lichen,
the white-streaked blue rocks, the broken icicles.
Now we are aware of red-flecked cheese scones and
blood pushing back into the ends of fingers. The air is steam
and light banter, the view is of humorous birthday cards
featuring gorillas and goldfish. The huge mural
presides like a ghost of what we came for, and have said
goodbye to, on the way to a long darkening drive
back to the artificial light, the narrow streets of our own
          bodies.

Piccadilly Gardens

children play in fluting streams
watched by men whose pants
are cast from cold wrought iron
to hide the tell-tale signs
that unleashed, punch 999
into frantic fathers' minds
who report, "robbery"
their exclusive property
coveted by other men's preying eyes

the green and purple kaleidoscopic clouds
of starlings' swirling evening cabaret
are years gone
replaced by metal birds
that roost with hard unblinking eye
static observers of urban life
the city turned voyeurs' paradise

in the cooling rain
night slides down
shadows shift and slink away
the children move like moths
drawn by bleeping squat machines
dispensing dreams of fame and unknown wealth
the 10p thrill of a neon pleasure dome
safer here, than in their homes

CHERYL PEARSON

Things That Can Be Broken

The road's back under boots and drills.
A bad tooth on a peach pit.
Silences, mornings. Sleeping-spells.
A star shivered up in a kicked bucket.

A sick fingernail, ridged with infection.
Mirrors and windows, a weak lock.
Sandcastle-keeps when the sea returns.
The braid of a fish-spine on a cutting block.

A Christmas wishbone in a death grip.
A voice under fathoms of bad news.
A soft, dropped apple, coughing its pips.
A slow snail under careless shoes.

A fast, a heart. A sapling split
by axes, lightning, rot, disease.
A talcumed grandmother's chalky hip.
Ice under boot-heels in a winter freeze.

A confidence, a promise. A fever. A skull.
A jilted bride, glittering like dew.
A horse's leg on a difficult hurdle.
Bread and circles. Me. You.

ROD TAME

St George is Cross

Three booze-crusaders,
Paddy, Andy and a boy called George
walk into a pub
and beat-up a Welshman.

Looking for Blackpool lights
on a Spanish night,
they toast the flag above the bar:

A flag
red as a sunburned skinhead,
white as an untanned torso,
and blue as the language of Brits frying on a costa,
basted in the grease of an all-day breakfast
and wearing Union Jack shorts.

A symbol
of unfulfilled lives, football-padded out
with the glories of false idols,
overpaid martyrs in Burberry plaid,
whose fans overstay their welcome at away games.

Paddy performs his party piece
to impress the senoritas;
ten tequilas all in a row.

lick, swallow, suck,
lick, swallow, suck
lick, swallow, suck
oh fuck

Stomach-lining is eroding,
its acid exploding forth

mixed with half-digested paella and chips.
Though, it is kind of a neat trick
how he catches it all in one pint pot,
a bullseye shot, not spilling a drop.

Andy rejects such high-brow seduction,
taking the lower tone.
He says, 'Hey Chiquita! Cop a load of this!'
whips up his kilt
and releases his Loch Ness monster.

Fails to live up to the legend.

Our third patron has had such fun
drinking in the midday sun.
Mad Dog George and his flagon of ale
finish a bout, ding ding,
barman calls time out.

Georgy-boy shouts,
'Oi Krauts, remember '66!'
Ironic, given his being born in '86
but he still gets a kick
from a victory long gone.

Tragic really, no boast more recent
and this behaviour indecent
results in a high-spirited game of hide and seek
in a crowded street.

Our heroic lads lose.

Hell-raising their way into a cell,
they can but dwell
on how three saints are reduced to knaves.

ROBIN IBBESON

The Pure Land

I had forgotten how we were then
the way I'd lie upon your grassy chest
shirt off, writing and reading
in that afternoon air
in that summer when I took too much Ecstasy

those happinesses and you
like brief fingers of a breeze on me
like breath

The mind cleared and present
growing into you

learning

It seemed like a season that would never change
but I left

and the branches became ink scratches
on sleepy pages
and empty colours

I forgot you
and could only recall a time when it was not how it had
           become.

Several years passed
in unfortunate and joyless winters
lonely the long unchange,
this impure land.

But now it is an early Easter
and this return
with no one else around

the strolling, mid-March
and thinking
remembering now, properly

those days

we are becoming again
in birdsong and new green
still cold but with character in the sun.

FERNANDO SMITH

Woman with No Toe

Jezebel
daughter of
Harold
broke the heel
of her shoe, snapped
her ankle
tac! tac!
like radio static and
remembered the foot curse
bestowed on her bloodline.

Back in Salford
a pronounced limp followed
a particularly ruthless
pedicure
and initiated a
funny walk
that attracted the attention
of the away fans
and a sexual deviant, up
on a day trip
from Rhyl.

Following her behind
a collapsing red-brick bookies
near the Lowry
he retched, upon
discovering
her quite dead

the result of slipping
on a discarded prawn
bhuna
and taking a toe
one Saturday afternoon.

Eleven Types of Vegetable

Something has got into the soil.
We were so careful, but
there it is. We won't be able
to get it out again. We have identified
eleven types of vegetable
which you should probably
avoid from now on. However,
for reasons of national
security, we are not at liberty
to name these vegetables specifically.

Our advice is to observe
your neighbours carefully.
Watch their shopping bags;
make a note of what goes in
and who comes out.
Look for clumps of hair
in the shrubbery, frequent
dentist appointments
and eventually, death.
If you have children,
encourage them to play indoors
and try not to have any more.
There is no need to panic. We are all
in this together.

The Suburbs

Between each impulse
of switching on and off the lights
he would regard the way
the furniture delved deeper into the walls,
the way the lithograph of a nude
shielded her nakedness behind glass
and only the moonlight throbbed
in the curtain folds.

The garden startled him
as he watched leaf shadows
dance in the bole of the tree.
He switched on the outer light –
floodlit the garden, until the sycamore
wound its long arm to impossible
heights in the sky –
silvery – luminous – silently manic.

He hid in the corner to watch,
wanting to flick on a switch –
make the dark room cosy,
the garden blind.
But the room had beckoned the moon,
its procession of ghosts,
that slipped endlessly in through the glass,
lined up on the parquet floor.

Neil Clarkson

Doing It for Yourself

I've been doing it for myself,
hacking at my cardboard hair,
fumbling in the darkness of my ears,
contorting to remove
all that has grown on my back.

I've been listening to tapes telling
people who teach people to read
how to teach people to read.
Now I'm teaching myself to read.

I've been carefully coming down the stairs,
wheel by wheel, pausing to look
at photographs of a better life.

I've been doing it for myself,
blowing a puff of powder in my eye,
sat in semi-darkness,
looking at jumbled red and green letters
without having to restrain my laughter.

I agonised for months, sharpening knives,
before I plunged in to get the gall stone.
Yes I skated in blood on the kitchen floor,
and there was pain,
but instead of a gall stone, out came a diamond.

CHRISTOPHER DOMMETT

Those Eyes

If I was asked the colour of my lovers eyes,
I'd pause;
think a while,
whilst struggling to picture.

You see our love is deeper than pigmentation,
superficial images almost disregarded,
those eyes to me are a prism spreading wide
opening up a world of rainbows.

Brighter life could not be lived without our joined stares,
though his glances display more colours than one
I know each look,
picture every image he's thinking deep,
all vividness bought forth to reality
even from the blankest expressions.

Often I smile though you are not present
but I know he feels its love,
your caress strokes me just within thoughts
carrying you everywhere I go.

Each time you laugh it tickles me,
lifts an already full heart to overflowing;

I gush for you,
spurt out jitters of emotion in deepness indescribable.

Touch me,
touch me now,
for I need those holds of forever,
arms that wrap around,

clenching together a once broken body
that you have slowly mended.

And if you must know
or have judged me as unobservant,
I'll tell you something;
the answer to that question,
for whatever reason
the meaningless obviously means something to you;

his eyes are brown.

Stevie Turner

Seagull-shaped

We meet at Taurus, the soft sofa cushions
dip in the middle, we are a biro-drawn
seagull shape, stretched over late September –
suspicious girlfriends, the dates we missed

We wonder if it's safe to fly on one beer
brush the static-locked hairs of our arms
together as we reach for our drinks, rise
on the wind of the incoming tide, glide

over a city time-lapsed through taxi windows
the back of your hand brushed down my face
I didn't notice – green moss, damp brick stains
on the back of my coat. I'd discover this later

Our love was a shoestring necklace, threaded
with sweet fudge screwed up in a white paper bag,
we made feasts from scraps in a rickety fridge
imprinted our bodies on the cool canvas of snow

a foot-deep in the meadow of the concrete forest;
friends warned us,
but we were never afraid of the wolf, the wolf,
we were never afraid of the wolf.

Charlotte Henson

Pharmacopoeia

A lunar leap in a freckle of time, she's a baby born on a leap
      year
god forbid. naked rat in a glass cage, she's loud,
demanding. despicable. your daddy always told you not to
      want –
that you'd only get hurt, your tiny feet
echoing in the halls of his experience.

mummy and daddy know best,
listen to what they tell you.
at six by a school desk, copying, copying,
always taught, never knowing better –
you hated and loved it and couldn't break the addiction.

couldn't slash that fatal addictive streak in your personality
that led you to a bar in your mid-twenties,
already painted brown by their experienced experience,
experience, experience; we know better.
tastefully dressed under none-too-tasteful lights
liquor burning in your veins like a steam train and unable to
      resist
just that element of superiority –
woke up in his bed feeling like meat.

mid-fifties with that bundle of cells
long banished from your womb.
'Joy' is not the word to describe something that keeps you up
      at night, louder than any banshee.
it was selfish screaming, annoying, not worth the pain,
straight to an adoption centre.

'she's not fit to be a mother,' they said, 'no one talks about
        their child like that.'
but really it was just how you felt – nothing to do with them.
        gossips.

in a badly lit study she is you and you are I,
we are they, from us they spawn
and grow
and die
but this is just pretty brain tissue
and she-you-I is just a fragment.
A plausible fragment,
but a fragment nevertheless,
and what are fragments worth?

Absolutely nothing.

Linda Cosgriff

Housewife
(With apologies to Eilean Ni Chuilleanain)

When this is over, said the housewife,
I mean to die: no retirement
for the likes of me.
No-one cares for my ironing.
Conversation is limited: 'Do your children visit?'

I intended to work, like my husband,
but the kitchen needed me.
Now, I polish my melamine counters, and cry.
I lie awake at night, count my pulse
and make plans to clean the cistern.

I once grew an orchard of tomatoes
in a pocket garden; slugs plundered it.
It was never summer when I had wet washing,
and my promise withered on the line.

Annie Clarkson

Valentine's Day

We will dress in jeans and heeled boots, meet in a renovated mill, brush its brick walls with our coats and let the dust settle.

We will drink elderflower cordial and hold our glasses in gloved hands, listening to people talk about love or anti-love.

We will wear lip gloss that nobody will smudge. We might kiss people on the cheek: friends, almost-friends, poets who stand in front of a mic with hands shaking or not shaking, their words echoing in the mill where years ago, a poet's words would be lost in the chatter of looms.

We will think about lost loves privately while everyone claps at another poem, and there might be a crack of sadness somewhere forgotten inside us. We might speak of it later when we step out into damp tarmac-streets where chimneys loom and the mill siren has long since stopped sounding the end of shifts.

We will walk in the shoes of girls who breathed cotton rather than poems, who laughed at boys from the weaving sheds, followed the backs of men with dye on their skin.

We will drink for the love we don't have yet, or the love we left behind, or the love we imagine for ourselves. And we might let go of this night.

Tough Old Boots

The costly forestry boots our kid insisted
warmed your twisted feet in the afterlife
didn't worry me in the slightest;
for you it was never about the price.

It wasn't your trainers which strained my heart,
or the leather uppers kicking me in the guts,
not the steel toe caps beating through healed scars.
Or even rubber wellies wading through the tears.

No slippered reminder of evening hours,
no sandals citing slipped away summers
no flimsy plimsolls linger to tease me,
frivolous footwear was never your thing.

Parting with the wrinkled fur lined riggers
feeling they would never again figure
in future footsteps left no aching
sole felt sore as I saw them departing.

It's knowing the old stiff soled walking boots,
dried dirt trapped in the tread from lakeside routes
laces flattened under loops, tongue lolling
… will not walk again over cold Helvellyn.

NEIL FAWCETT

Asylum

With each drag the man's sleeve shifted
to show dark skin, pitted with deep
white scars; bowls of cooled craters hot
with old pain. I think of Helen.

She had skin like silk, softly tanned
by the summer of '76
with fine, fair hairs that melted first,
curling crisp in the glowing heat.

I ask the interpreter about
the scars. 'Self inflicted,' she said.
'It's not uncommon, the pain blinds,
briefly, the mind's eye.'

It started with a pound note, a
match and a crumpled cigarette.
I didn't smoke so her fag felt
awkward between my finger and thumb.

It was her idea. The trick
was to wrap the note around her
slender wrist, drag on the fag and
burn a hole before she fainted.

'He says they made him watch her die.
Held her high on a bayonet.
Passing her one to the other
Laughing, laughing, laughing, laughing.'

I sit across the table from
a brown-skinned scarred man,
who reminds me of the girl
I've not tortured for twenty years.

All Smiles Ride with Me

it's the little moments that i have come to adore

the unexpected kink of the lips before the kiss
the oopsy grin of mischief revelling on the baby-faced
      morning
the polite nod that blossoms into a full hello

comrades
if i should fail
and this diary survives me
i want to be remembered as the first of our kind to witness
      this humanity
especially
as we know i was among our strongest doubters before i
      arrived

even as i write i can feel myself changed
my fingertips are aching
to go back out and explore afresh
the spectacular systems of their lives
to revisit the same precious jolting of sensation
until it fixes itself in the heart of my circuits

i think it was the lovers that first turned me
i saw their eyes widen from across a room
then a brightening
the booting of expressions
newly-borne teeth
beckoning with warm invitation

there were other highs
the beauty that glittered with modest surprise

the proud champion and his father
relaxing into reckless laughter
and the two good friends who barely moved a muscle
but still signalled   i know i know

tomorrow i will radio back to base
i will happily report that we got it wrong

down here
there really are flickering lights as far as the eye can see

admittedly
collecting samples has been a problem
so i am opening the doors as far as they will go
i am painting myself a wonderful banner too

six foot lettering
in lipstick
red
it reads

all   smiles   ride   with   me

BEN WILLEMS

No Bins

On Crofton Street
a driveway's closed black gates
with words

NO BINS
in thick white paint.

Wonder... do they mean
NO BINS
on the pavement here
in front of the closed black gates
underneath the words

NO BINS
in thick white paint?

Where, as it happens, about
15 bins, of various colours, congregate.

CORA GREENHILL

Desert Trade

Even the sky is dust.
Walls and streets bleached
mud: all shades of beige.

He seats himself before us,
a pool of blues, unwinds
a river of indigo from his face,
which shines like oil,
purple with dye that's bled.

Long, tapered fingers flash
their rings as he unpacks
treasure from crumpled calico:
amber, hammered silver,
polished camel teeth.

The bargain made, we pay. He stays.
Expectant. The ceremony of trade
is incomplete. I grope around
for gifts. Find soap, in hotel wrappers.

His sneer reveals gold teeth.
'Tuareg women don't use soap.
Just oil.' A gleaming
finger pokes my flesh, its shades
of beige. As if its pigment
had been lost by washing.

JANET LOVERSEED

Small Doses of Shadow

When her lover died, Abigail wanted
sedatives to help her sleep her grief away
but her doctor said 'No, Abigail,
I'd like you to take small doses of shadow.
They're better for you. But not the synthetic
sort you can buy at the pharmacy
or the stale shadows lurking in your bedroom
in the semi-dark. The freshest shadows
found in sunlight: leaves dancing
on the bark of a tree, clouds over hills,
fields or the sea. And of your own
body, striding with long steps
towards the future.'

She was puzzled by these strange instructions
but she tried to do as the doctor said.
On bright days she sought her dose of shadow
out of doors. On dull days she lit her house
with lamps and watched the shadows of her hands
clasp each other on the white walls. She knew
her dose should be small but she was becoming
addicted. The well-defined dark forms
and soft grey shapes all gave her great joy.
When she looked at them she felt her eyes widen
at what they saw. The shadow of a bird
moved her most. She wanted more: its shining eye,
wing-draught, heartbeat, song.

Princess

She was not a real princess.
On the corner of Midnight and Spirit,
achingly sober, shaved arm pits,
smiling a bent moon beam,
paid
to stand
and wait.

You could have seen she was no princess
in the snow white of her eye
when "he" told her, *'You are a princess.'*
when "he" told her, 'Show some thigh.
Flip that frown. Wake up, Beauty,
smell the coffee liqueur.
Half price booze! We are open till four.
Shout it loud! Make me proud.
Show some shoulder. Lose that bra.
Bring our lads in. Fill my bar.'

But she didn't feel like a princess
on the corner of Midnight and Spilled Spirit Staining
fumbling out flyers.
Smiling.
Smiling.

She felt like an iceberg with an American accent,
an origami swan made from unpaid bills
paid
to stand
and wait.

This world will never want her skills.
She could make a Crystal Castle with pasta and glue,

knew twelve ways to cheat at a Rubik's Cube,
could create voices for pencils
but
she worked for a bar
in a strapless bra
on the corner of Midnight and Empty.

And then seven little men
got too close.
Boozy,
Schmoozy,
Handsy, Shouty,
Licky, Pukey and Punch
said hello,

'Hi... ho!'

'Nice legs. When do they open?'
'D'you like chicken? This cock'll have you chokin'.'
'Don't put out your goods if you're not selling too.'
'If you were my daughter, I would still be bathing you.'

She was no princess.
Loyal to her boss, her Prince Harming,
she faced these little men,
these mice disguised as stallions,
rodents wrapped in beer-sticky manes.
'Neigh. Squeak! Neigh.'
The customer isn't always bright

but she was.

Brighter than any crown.
That was the day she walked away.

She walked away
and their taunts turned to fairy dust,
insults dissolved

like shadows clouding into candy floss.
She walked away
body full of sunrise,
her skin a goose bump farm.
Honk! Honk!
She cleared the road!
Ripped down the corner of Midnight.
Spirit of Kate Bush, Lionheart and twilight.
Wow – Wow – Wowed through morning,
Spirit to Swift Wind,
blizzards of light hope quivered her lungs.
Rubik's cube squares flitted free at her feet
like Billie Jean!

Now,
she might be inventing the rechargeable biro.
Might bake the first daffodil pie.
She might have become a princess...
or anything.

CAROLE OGDEN

Naked Ladies Kissing

A girl in a bluebottle coat scuttles by,
head down, rushing into town.
She has shiny hair, shuttered eyes and sensible shoes:
a girl whose parents would be proud.

A man in a Plasticine hat appears,
wearing a tie he borrowed from a friend.
Loud, tired and cheap, he will keep it
long after the end of the friendship.

By the frown of a streetlight,
Mr Oversight sings his swansong.
Shuffling along and tapping his toes
to a tune only he knows,
clicking his over-long fingers.

On the other side of the road
stands the nuclear family,
using mobile phones to keep in touch.
They send each other photos
of their smiling faces.

Rain soaks, like a memory,
into the skins of the paper children,
huddling against tall walls.
Unnoticed, they slip, once more,
back between the cracks in the road.

The world passes by
under the influence of billboards
and naked ladies kissing.

JOYCE REED

Changes

In the purity of the pealed morning,
towers across fields and fen
are gossiping about Plain Bob and Grandsire Triples.

The swinging sallies rise and fall,
gripped to the call
of 'treble going – she's gone.'

Bare arms muscle to the up and down of it,
the sweat of it, with muddied minds of Saturday
now clarified as the buttery beams of belfry light
through latticed slats.

No-one can still lie in dreams
in the lee of these churches
where the stones vibrate to worship's marshalling.

And I hear, but do not heed
the summons of the iron bells,
as my faith flaps like the precinct pigeons
on the lying wind.

ANGELA SMITH

The City Sweats

The city sweats
Chip fat and beer.
Stripped of t-shirts
Winter pale chests and backs
Turn wincing red.

The city sweats
Perfume and alcopops.
Like dancing flowers
The young women –
As bright
And as ephemeral.

The city sweats
Musky pheromones.
You can almost taste
Salt tinged skin
Gleaming in the sunlight.

The city sweats
Sour milk and frustration.
In wordless fury
The infant on the bus
Protests the heat.

The city sweats
Cappuccinos and poems,
Lethargic lust,
Tears and gossip,
And finally,
Blessedly,
The city sweats
Rain.

Rachel McGladdery

Kiting It

I'm having to trust the universe today.
It stretches in the sky, fine and taut and
it looks like promise,
but I have the stars to juggle
and they're fiddly
and sharp cornered.
My view is small (I guess)
but it's tenting so far,
the stitch is holding.
And I
am trusting, tight thin, wire,
tied right around my fingers.
I'm kiting it,
I'm holding up the sky.

Rosie Lugosi

Dignity

Throwing up over the consultant
when he asks you how you're feeling.
Throwing up
so hard it comes out of your nose.
Acquiring the skill of throwing up accurately.

Farting.
Discovering that chemo farts are more powerful than
      Semtex
and can clear a room just as effectively.

Saying, I don't need a Zimmer frame to get to the bathroom!
Then falling into a chemical waste bin
and getting a two-inch scar on your forehead.

Getting out of bed and showing the whole ward
and their relatives your knickers
except you aren't wearing any.

Calling for a commode
during visiting hours
although everyone can hear through the paper curtain
and everyone can smell.

Fainting.
Coming round on the bathroom floor
wringing wet, stark naked and stretched out
under the eyes of seven nurses who've had to kick the door
      down.

Tolerating strangers
who whisper you're so brave.
Resisting the urge to deck them.

Going bald.
Watching your tits shrivel to the size of peanuts
and your arse go flat as a burst paper bag.

Begging
for another shot of morphine
even though you had one half an hour ago
even though you know they'll say no, you have to wait.

Remaining polite
when a close friend
drops off the face of the Earth
when you tell him your diagnosis.
Remaining polite
when the same close friend
reappears when you are better
and acts like nothing's happened.
Remaining polite
when people cross a room
in case you talk to them about it.

Wearing long sleeves in June
to cover up the scarlet tracklines
chemotherapy has etched from wrist to elbow.
Rolling up those sleeves to show them off as battle scars.
Learning to stare back.
Wearing a feeding tube up your nose.
Learning to stare back.

Refusing to wear the prescription wig
that makes you look like you've got cancer.
Refusing to wear the cheerful floral scarf
that makes you look like you've got cancer.

Standing up, falling over.
Standing up, falling over.
Standing up, hanging onto the arm of the sofa, the edge of
    the table,

grabbing at furniture in a dot-to-dot of small stages.
Waddling to the kitchen on a toddler's unsteady legs.
Making a cup of tea unaided.
Eating your first solid food in three months.

Standing up
and saying I've got cancer
without need, without self-pity.
Standing up
and saying I'm clear.

Julia Deakin

Coasting

Sometimes momentarily
you're back there doing Geography,
the rows of pine tables warm,
the long room Thursday-stuffy
and the strip lights bright
against the outside blur
of brick and sodium, the looming fog
cocooning, bandaging,
erasing Manchester

to leave a kind of no man's land
of safety in the Philip's High School Atlas
open at Peru, Australia, the Great Lakes,
each with their oyster edges to be traced,
ink pens coaxed
towards that blissful payoff
with a flat blue crayon. That frill –
making the exercise book
look three dimensional.

So easy then, it seemed, to sail
above the fog to lands of clarity,
neat blue boundaries
which sloped off evenly
to clear blue seas.
Time and a steady hand
all you'd need
to make the whole world safe.

The Waiting

I steal a pen from a stationery shop
Stroll the dark corridors of memory
Become jealous of a friend's laughter
Think about a soap star's armpit
Smash a window in anger
Watch a dog lick his bollocks
Kill a slug
Juggle unsuccessfully with gravity

I sleep on the edge of a cloud
See pink fuzz on a clover
Burn a bed behind a house
Offer a girl her first cigarette
Ejaculate on a piano
Make fun of God-fearing people
Walk the nine circles
Throw ink at the moon

I dream of swans
Answer questions with "truth hurts"
I count down the days
I bang in the nails

Kay Boardman

Apple Pie

You bend over the mixing bowl
pummelling, flour, fat and sugar.
Calloused knuckles labour on,
as accustomed to looms and bobbins
as they are to the soft yielding dough.

Jim Reeves croons in the background.
Children squeal from the coal shed,
its warm ebony dust mingling with
the fractured sound and light.
As you knead, pummel and knead
virginal puffs of flour dissipate in the cacophony of sound
locked tight in your head like goods in your well-stocked
          pantry.

Memory takes you back
to when you danced at the Palais
with gravy browning seams on the back of your legs.
To when you had enough money for a quarter of bacon
and a pound of best butter.
To a time when there were no children,
only a handsome Brylcreemed man
who was mesmerised by your smile.

The kneading is done.
The pastry deposited without struggle
on to a chipped earthenware plate
with faded figures in a firm embrace.
Apples drop lazily in the case,
the pastry lid is pressed on.
A shower of sugar makes the dome complete.

Pie bakes, Jim croons, children squeal,
and the memories of mislaid times
float away with the pungent smell of sweet baked apples.

For Your Information

Doors opening.
Please choose one of the following…
Unexpected item in the bagging area
please remove yourself before continuing.
Passengers should refrain from
smoking in the smoking area.
Passengers should also refrain from
damaging vehicles whilst at this station
for your safety
Cash may be removed
or damaged by
the security services.
Passengers are not permitted
anywhere within the station building
Doors closing
due to today's wet weather
this lift has been cancelled
Doors opening.
Customers are reminded
not to go down on
unaccompanied passengers.
Your attention please
this announcement
has been cancelled.

It is not permitted to
cycle, roller skate, smoke,
go up, go down,
enter vehicles, exit vehicles,
enter or leave
whilst at this station.

Passengers are advised
not to go down to the woods today
we apologize for any inconvenience
this has caused you
we are sorry
we are sorry
we are so
sorry
sorry
sorry
doors
closing
dzzz

My Son Climbing

He's a lover of these tilted embraces:
the slim foothold, the fingertip clinch,
these plights of breath, and trials of grip,
these archings and anxious reachings,
the impossible angles and turns of ligament,
the locked wrist, the arched hip, the lurching
for one leg-cleaving hour on the rock –
for the inch-of-height, for the out-of-reach.
He turns his ear to the chest of the cliff
his arms splayed like a sleeping baby.
Then he's off, cutting his teeth on these faces,
breaking his nails on the flanks
of death-drops and cleft intimacies.

Above him the shape of a man or a stone
and what it is that will cut its teeth on him.
Wind-pocked and scree-shanked by loose time
I play out a touch more slack on the belay
as he pulls on absence and breaches gaps.
Taut in my fingers – something of his weight.

BELINDA JOHNSTON

Lily Street

Terraced houses stand stern.
Their windows solemn –
dressed with wincing cats:
tails ratty from relentless rain.

Dustbins guard alleyways
and chomp on the heads
of displaced leaves.

Meanwhile, the Cross Keys
pub sign squeals
for custom, as raincoats
skirt her entrance,

in exchange for take-outs
that suck in air from
inside plastic bags.

STEPHEN M HORNBY

A Good Goodbye

There are many ways to say goodbye.
I could revisit old loves, and emboldened by departure,
tell them the other half of the truths that cowardice silenced.
I could sit in places ripened by sentiment to the point of
        rotting
and conjure the casual comedies of quotidian life.
I could hold a fin de siècle party, and full of solipsistic angst
beatify moments of random, heightened closeness.

I could remember who I was.

But, I think it's best done gently,
like a moment's distraction to the sound of distant song.

The choice to go is always a form of rejection.
And it is met with real tears or feigned indifference.
The severance a litmus paper of all that we felt,
and of all that we did not feel, shockingly visible.

I have been secretly leaving for over two years now,
and the partings have barely been noticed.
Even as they have piled one on top of one another,
attenuating me to little more than a hearty ghost.

I have slipped away like
the scent from cut roses,
youth from a face,
warmth from a blanket.

Until suddenly,

there is just a space,
but not a void.

Only a few people will recall me going: those I love.
And they will be with me on the journey anyway.
It's about those whom I just quite liked:
they are the real losses, the real departures.
And for them,
I think it's best done.
Gently.

TOM GEORGE

Careless Wispa

Full of eastern promise you were silkily sublime
I was just a Drifter and I didn't have a Dime
Feeling rather Flake-y, I asked you for a date
Luckily you said 'Ok, I'll meet you After Eight'

It was such a trendy place – the Biggest Ever Bar
Every single Revel-ler was looking like a Star
You turned up looking luscious and gave me such a Twirl
And when I saw thoSenickers, you had to be my girl

The Topic of discussion was neither there nor here
After half an hour I heard you Wispa in my ear
Is there any Riesen for us to even stay?
I took you back to my place
We went the Milky Way

I'd dream about you constantly
Through work and rest and play
I couldn't stand to let you go a Waifa half a day
We had a secret recipe for sensual sexcess
But in each other's pockets we became a sticky mess

See, you may like the like the wrapper
But what lies underneath?
I thought you were a fondant but you nearly broke my teeth
You looked so very precious, I thought you were All Gold
It took me time to realise that you were just plain cold

You left me feeling bitter about those heart-shaped lies
You said it all with Roses but never with your eyes
I gave you presents, you were only faKin der Surprise
And then you'd go and take the piss
And call me Mr Fun Size

I never took Time Out to work out just what made you tick
I realised I'd had enough, you'd made me feel sick
A thin veneer of confidence was jettisoned that day
Like silver paper, crumpled up and cruelly tossed away

So, passion-hungry browsers, be careful what you choose
And linger at love's counter, lest you should buy the blues
I got into the healthy stuff – bought myself a wok
Now you should see my social diary – it's choc-a-block!

Because It Was Beautiful:
The Giving Birth

Beseech is not the word,
someone said. Too archaic. Dramatic.
Another with a mild disapproval
read it as a second language expert
and concluded the font to be italic.
So, I put my hands on the steering wheel
and turned west
for as I understood,
it should fit the context
outside my construct.

Yet I'm always inclined to go
where the sun rises
where the shadow of my short vowels
intend to woo the colossal consonants
like litanies dressed in morning dews
to put clothiz on the chilidrin
before they walk away from their motherly chimes.
But the chilidrin put their porcelain shoes on.
They stumble.
    They stutter.
  And they keep on.
Because the children should fit the context
outside their homely construct
to be understood. Correct?

SARAH MILLER

The Hard Nature of Crows

They have the hard nature of crows
dark hooded shapes
pecking over the wasteland
preening
squawking at any
that wander
onto their territory
plucking out eyes
ripping flesh
blackening the sky of whole estates
I try not to judge them
but I have seen their claws
sharpened knives
machetes
bragging the air
like stuttering semi-automatics.
They have tarred and feathered their nests.
They have made their own bombs.
I know they can't help it
they are just following their nature
and nature is hard
stray chicks are vulnerable
easy prey
picked off
in ragged acts of aggression
I know it's not their fault
they have the hard nature of crows
but I know how they earned their collective name
yes, I know why they call them a murder.

New Focus

Sad I could not shift the gloom
from his half-forbidding home,
opaque with a lifetime's clutter –
grey plants, hard furniture,
book fust and pictures
of the dead wife wasting –
we had a night of jostling
our chalky bodies round the bed
that creaked as though releasing
a memory, slowly.

Later, walking back to the station,
the sun's far-reeling eye
took hope's place, almost blinding
while I tried to keep from turning back,
from assuming the role of broken planet
waiting for its late star's orbit.

Lucifer Lightbringer

Lucifer Lightbringer
> *once-beloved of God!*
lived in a mid-terrace in Moss Side
a two-up two-down the colour of hot coals
rented a room to a misfit cast of wayfaring strangers;
poets and prophets just passing through.

Lucifer Morningstar
> *the Un-Holiest of Holies!*
spoke in whispers and off-key rosaries
charmed stray cats and small children
and grew tiny Trees of Knowledge
in the ragged back garden of a man with midnight skin
and a smile as smooth as margarine

Lucifer Split-Tongue
> *harbinger of Phosphorus and Lumen!*
sipped slow pints in the Claremont
slipped whispers and resentment and expectation
into the ears of old men
debated the origins of his name with a pixie-faced lady
transubstantiated a pint of Diamond lager
and left the barman a golden calf

Lucifer Old Spit
> *patron saint of scapegoats!*
unbuttoned abandon on the side of a canal
blew a filmmaker in his forty-fifth year
loved an installation artist on the south side of Whalley
        Range

called sirens and succubae to sing sweet songs down the
        alleyway
bought them cups of coffee at Jam Street in the morning

Lucifer Leatherheart
        first of all serpents!
blessed bottles of After Shock
played dress-up with a poet with oil slick hair
teetered on high heels in Fallowfield
never said no to a party
screeched and squealed with ecstasy when bent over by
        scallies
and promptly returned the favour.

Lucifer Darkest-Hour
        (the only one to give Jesus any options)
lost a finger when The Printworks was rebranded
lost two teeth on the big wheel
lost his left hand in the Hacienda Apartments
lost his sight when the Basement burned down
lost his train of thought at every new Costa Coffee staring
        back at him
and thought about moving to Liverpool.

Simplicity

Alone, and the stroke of my pen on the page
is the dance,
the fragile escape of bubbles:
two, three rising,
is that search for connection,
the tracing of someone's words long ago
from some lost age,
is the hope of a spark,
is the blaze of that blinded reach in the dark,
is that desperate grasp
of that last burnt full stop
and the drop
of surrendering pen in a graceless arc.

And if one reaching out in the dark of sleep,
one man in a crowd, or one, on the brink, calling out loud
in search of just one thing (*love?*)
should feel, just-not-enough,
the whisper, the tentative connection
like the brush of bubble skin,
then why not here? why not now?
when the hope of that feeling,
that trying to understand
is the most basically human,
the most distant and sudden,
and the pen and the paper are that purest collision –
the simple touch of hands.

…

But I stand
and I leave the pen
and I leave the room,

and the complicated whirl of life in cartoon slides is bright
        and dizzying,
and there are many things for which we search
but none that simple, none that pure.

.   .   .

Behind closed doors, the pen and the paper,
a stolen moment of humanity: the breeze rolls the nib,
the ink flows
and the bubble cheeks kiss,
bump then part
spiral out up
away
but still, for that one second,
that momentary touch of skin to skin,
that almost not there press
of locked-in air,
that simplest rare occurrence: touch
(outside and in)
their malleable selves carry the mark
of the other's sudden skin.

FRANCESCA PRIDHAM

In the Kitchen

Suddenly the room is very orange
and I can see where the lines have blurred
between the ceiling and the wall.
Even the bowl in the sink is orange.

Years later I'm told orange
is an immature colour;
your kitchens are always orange.

I am in the night.
I thought you were with me.
The millpond like my head
lies in the darkness outside the window
where the curtains have not been drawn.
We have driven together
I have stopped at the pub and asked the way,
the lights blinding the answer they gave,
the noise smarting in my ears.

He has been strip searched and left in a room.

The bed was bare. There were no sheets.
His belt was taken away from him. His money taken.
His pockets emptied.

The whole ache of my childhood
to give you space
to give you freedom from him
and now I hear you say
I love him why have they,
why have you taken him away.

I try to listen and then I try not to listen
so that I can stay. At least I hope my body in the room
is comfort though your words have
taken my world and thrown it all away.

June '92

He came in through the bathroom window,
cracked it with the peak of a knuckle
or the beak of a rock, a small
incision, enough to reach in
and open up a door
for a crawler.

He made a mess on the tiles, soap and
shaving foam knocked from the sill,
the gunk of spittle from the toothbrush cup
spilled over splinters of glass.

He had a choice of treasure chests
on the landing, but I suppose
he chose the closest, and in our room
exposed the innards of drawers and wardrobes,
pulling out tights like intestines
and throwing shirts and pants
aside, scattering sex debris across the floor.

He took the passports naturally, a handful
of jewellery and the present for Peter,
you can see where he sat
on the bed and unwrapped it,
shards of blue paper
dropped on the duvet,
I wonder if he smiled and said thanks
to the silence, just what I wanted, best Christmas ever.

He moved through our rooms to
quench his quick lust, filled his sack up
with gifts for the season: a laptop,

an Xbox, a TV, a watch,
for every item taken
a shock of space, an outline of dust.

He drank a beer in the kitchen, shifted
the seats for legs-up comfort and
ate a mince pie on the side, a gored
slice grinning on the table.

He wrote a note in the lounge, it says
sorry I did this. dan, and he placed it by
an open photo album, snaps from
ten years ago, and there's a
gap on the page, and the caption under the
blankness reads June '92, and I cannot
remember what the picture was of.

STEPHEN SUNDERLAND

Accident

I heard her say it –
how she'd only ever wanted a dog.
She put out her cigarette, anyhow;
hunkered down for the big push.

I bide my time here,
paws a-scutter in the foam bath;
hearing talk of three-wheelers
on glass-clicking sunny afternoons in spring;

and dream of a parliament of dogs,
preside over reasoned debate
about thought, health, good deeds;
and how to win her back.

But she cannot hear me, will not hear me;
no matter how hard I bark or whine;
how much my wise companions show me
their howly love of all things dog.

I test the flavours she has in store for me
the spicy, the bitter, the smoked;
second guess my place
in the populated kingdom;

learn of missiles and mortgages;
the price of loving, the cost of not;
the many ways to flee down side alleys
to the special place beyond words and deeds.

There is more in heaven and earth;
my symphony of yelps confirms it.
When I spring forth there will be hell to pay.
This much I know.

Electricity

Today the sun defies the rain
Shines on the street, cuts through
The morning like an overheard
Five a.m. whistle or the scent
And ghost-buzz of post-storm air
Reigns in the silence, spreads it over
The flimsy skin of these early hours
Yearns to stretch, bend its blank rays,
Dazzle into ears all cut-throat and noiseless
Callous sunrise rejects gravity and blazes and blazes
Then sputters as it sparkles
Flickers like jewels hidden beneath beetle wings
And sinks into the loudest shadow

Day Out

as the edge of the sea
sands my toenails down
I ask

why that man sat beside me
is still there

whether that long-boned girl
with the slow-motion run
is mine

are they related?

the waves crashing together
and the trees
going mad in my garden

are they related
or am I finally cracking up

and as the sea seeps through
the crack in my eye

I run to keep up
with the man and the girl.

CHRIS STEVENSON

Path

... and then running through the derrydown,
intermittent views of valleys came about,
cherry red in autumn, cloth and leaf,
the sun sparks on the river mouth.

... a bird, unseen, tripped across my path,
just the voice disappearing turned my head,
a ghost surely of one grey feather,
a voice from the past, frozen, dead.

... the path descends in cracking bracken,
splintering shards, sliding stones,
the prospect under clouds before me,
one of travellers' whitening bones.

... for ahead of me I hear their voices,
hear their movement, sliding down,
these valley sides still inspire the dead,
and hold my feet, and wait for me now.

... there's nothing here, I was nothing then,
pretend I'm gone, or I never came,
slipping on shards I will fall away,
a hollow path under a gentle rain.

EMMA DECENT

Naked

We know each other naked.
Curve of buttock
the slope of chest
curl of pelvis
the softness of inner skin.
Details of body only a lover knows.

With you
nakedness is safe
easy
not perilous exposure
Like oneness
Like grown-ups doing grown-up things.

No embarrassment or vulnerability
in our bodies,
Only delight,
gleeful familiarity,
connection,
recognition
passion
home.

Nakedly one
in our lustful loving
Our loving lust.
Perfect physical click.

But I never see you... Naked.
Shedding clothes on your way to a shower
Padding round the house between bath and bed
Clipping your toes, cleaning your teeth.

We take off our clothes
and we know each other
Know each other's touch and response,
what makes us gasp,
breathe hard.
You know the soft hairs on my back
I know the taste of your skin,
the weight of you upon me.

But you don't know me... Naked.
Exposed
alone
snot-faced and bewildered.
You don't know what makes me... Dance
sing out loud
rage
give up.

We don't know each other naked,
raw, unclothed and undefended.
The parts we don't show –
vulnerabilities
the secrets and shame
pain and self-doubt
hopes and dreams –
No.
We keep these hidden
behind our beautiful
sexy
adult
naked bodies.

Embarrassed,
ashamed,
we turn away
from indecent exposure
of self and soul.
Such nakedness,
we haven't the heart for.

Harry Matthews

According to John

Strokes of mathematical modelling
and differential equations,
add to the sub-aquatic implications
of the sloshing of liquids.

So says Accordion John
who loves to play improvised
laments in his retirement.

He's busking on Oxford Road
and cries: 'Students these days!'
(They asked him for 50p,
but with student fees gone up
he's not surprised.)

He tells me he looks for algorithms in
pigeon motions in Chorlton lime trees.
Now at the bowling green,
old time lyrics fill the air
like protest songs.

Ushered from the pub,
he strikes up nostalgic
with a wheel-bound pensioner
who knew the blitz.

I walk with him up the Wilbraham Road.
He ponders the "curse of dimensionality",
a problem my broken mind
cannot engage with
in practical terms,
for solving the application
of the sloshing of liquids.

Take —

An exam. Ages to get ready. Sugar in tea.
An interest. A chance. Your clothes off. Virginity.
The long view. Me as your lawful wedded.
This ring. Vows. The last slice of cake.
Us as you find us. Each day as it comes.
Your time.
Offence. The piss. Umbrage.
No prisoners. Hostages.
That. It on the chin.
Pains.
My advice. Two tablets every four hours.
A chair. Five. Time out. A deep breath.
A minute to calm down. A moment to reflect.
Out. Some time off. A break. It from me.
It one day at a time. It easy. Away.
Lessons in a foreign language. A holiday.
Flight.
My breath away. Care. A lover. Me as I am.
A mental photograph of you smiling.
My hand. Pleasure in it. Heart.

Fokkina McDonnell

Joan

One of the girls I went to college with
was Joan, who'd left home early.

She smoked Gauloises, had a stubborn
streak, wanted to study philosophy.

We thought she was depressed; she cut
herself and once put out a cigarette on her arm.

I wish I'd asked her why. I can see her now
with that hair cropped short, staring straight ahead.

People shouting, the smoke, the crackling fire.
Too hot, I need to step back.

Lucy Winrow

Gremlins

For months we inhabited
Those wet bricks below the city
Its passages of darkness
With our view of the still black sewer
Gliding thickly by like treacle
We hid among the rats
The bats, the pigeons
Who huddled up high
And watched us from ledges
Of bright phosphorous shit
While their feet rotted

Once a swan appeared like an angel
We kissed like trolls down there
The wet drip was relentless
Made a moist mossy spike
Down the wall
It kept me awake at night
The only signs of the world up there
Came down pipes, through vents
The bitter whoosh of car exhausts
The heavy press of fat black tyres
The clip of footsteps overhead

We ventured out only at night
Where we gleamed in streetlights
Picked out by strobes
In the corners of dusky clubs
My lips rounded on cold glass
Music throbbing down my arm
But inside I was starting to rot
So I stopped going out at night

Stopped going down there
And if I'm honest
I left you down there to rot

Now I stay indoors at night
Avoid the places we used to go
The smell of sour beer and sweat
I go out in the cold bright day
I walk alone and with purpose
Careful to avoid the grates
Too afraid to look down there
And see your pale eyes
Staring up at me
Through the bars

And I continue to rot.

GEMMA LEES

My Grandma Painted Her Eyebrows On

My grandma painted her eyebrows on
And lived in a palace full of gold
She had a turret just like Rapunzel
And maybe a horse and carriage

My grandma painted her eyebrows on
And looked like a lady from a black and white film
She had gowns and beads, long, long gloves
And grew special purple hair

My grandma painted her eyebrows on
And never made me drink flat lemonade
Sometimes she had to breathe into a special machine
But she was never too tired to play

My grandma painted her eyebrows on
She would have won all the glamorous gran competitions
        hands down
Other grandmas just sat knitting and drinking tea
Not mine
My grandma painted her eyebrows on

Staff Room

Nine Maid Marians
in unmarked iron suits;
an overlapping brood.

Saplings fruiting each semester
into rooted trees.

Vanishing biscuits and pens
amidst the cackle of birds
that pick through books and bags.

Their room
Their nest
Their hive

The bell —
and in the swell they rise
and fly to war,
down corridors
in tight formation.

DERMOT GLENNON

Smashed Fragments Huddled for Warmth

Beneath a yawning ambivalent sky
Thynne Street shivers in the early dark
broken bits of Britain stir
and walk out scarf wrapped
coughing like gypsies dead from living
crackles scattered on a floor of frost
where life is a Londis of use-by dates
and Mars bar breakfasts bought in haste
choking on the fumes of the Bank Quay station
fragranced by soap factory smoke.

Frost and hail trail footprints grey
beneath a cold and stone-washed sky
and lies like words:
community, and
centre
as hid by ugly blankets of smog-black brickwork
who knows what lives are lived and died
families struggle
food and clothing
toys and drugs
Muslim clothing white hat white trousers
walking the hail caked streets to mosque.

Beneath a yawning ambivalent sky
morning has broken – like the first nose
of night-time's heated angry debacle
overtired blue wicked one-a-penny
one-a-penny
wicked by the bottle
waking to recriminate on who said what and why
and why indeed

wicked by the bottle load
ten-a-penny
ten-a-penny
shut your noise.

Beneath a yawning ambivalent sky
broken bits of Britain stir
and make their shivering faltering walks
as heat escapes their very bones
to who knows where – who cares
to idle bag lady vagrant stand about
town centre hang out window shop
and dream a dream and plan escape
each broken piece of Britain dreams
beneath a yawning ambivalent sky
of gluing our lives together again
each fragment fastened to the next
with approximations to love.

MICHELLE PARAMANANTHAM

Studying the Sky this Month

studying the sky this month
we measured the actual brightness
the motion of molecules; the heat given off
coming to the conclusion that, in everything,
all our surface material
is fading slightly
and keeps fading

JOY FRANCE

Toast

I'm the bread. You're the toaster.
You get turned on every evening, at ten.
Sometimes I am ready, sliced.
White. Thick. Very easy.
I go down and you slowly start to turn me brown, then
PING!
You pop too soon – and I am left pale and wan and wanting.

Oh sweet recollection of when I was fresh baked, rough cut
and you toasted me daily to butter-oozing perfection.
But now I am same old, same old, Danish Light.
Calorie counted, air filled, bland brand shite.
We barely touch before I'm snatched away,
day, after day, after day – until today.
TODAY I was granary. Seeded. Lumpy. Chunky.
Your heat swelled every fibre
as I pushed against your bars.
I was singed glory and you strained to rise.
'FZZZZZZ'
Metal knife, power surged down wires
and your life... Expired.

So here I wait in anticipation
of a flirtatious communication
with a brand new model.
Sleek. Silver. Stainless steel. Ripe for seduction.
With cool to the touch body. Extra long slots. And... Reheat
        function!

GARETH TWOSE

Man on Roof in Gun Siege

The clouds have drifted all summer
running away from time
coming apart like wet tissue

Pale skin seen and touched,
breath brushing my face
she, who moved away

I listen to the clouds say:
we chase the passing sky

Rhiannon L Cree

Grandmère

The speckled plate has worked loose from the flyleaf:
"à Mlle L. Tarriér
le premier prix d'Anglais
Guéret, le 28 Juillet 1902"

She is stepping from the must and beeswax of the Lycée
into a day drunk with sunshine.
She and the pulsing cicadas
are the only things still moving in this heat,
though the sweep of her skirts startles brown lizards
into the cracks of the Place.
She keeps to the shadows of the plane trees,
winds past the quietly baking church,
the sleeping boulangerie and the slanted alleys
to where the rush of the weir
frees her to voyage.

She is promenading with her tall Scot
along the harbour wall – pre-war Alexandria,
avant-garde, bright and brittle.
She has a voice
good enough for opera, they tell her.
She airs it at select soirées,
swaps stories and rivalries under the parasols.

A shot splinters her world.

She is packing her grief and madness tight
in the leather trunk, taking the three lost children
back to their father's island,
enshrining him in page after page of green ink
in that fin de siècle French hand
with which later she steers

Winston's course through the war,
(did he ever read those earnest reams?)
holding herself so rigid her limbs freeze.

And here, at the last, she is sitting
in her marcasite earrings and tartan shawl,
a feathered sliver of chic on her scant grey hair,
enthroned in her wheelchair,
with the face of a proud old marquise.

"à Marguérite Louise Tarriér
le premier prix d'Anglais"

DAVE MORGAN

Lines Written in Tudor House on the 30th Anniversary of the Death of John Lennon

Hey Johnnie
You hook-nosed bastard
You made specs sexy
And played a mean Rickenbacker
Attention seeking nihilist
Gobshite Scouser
Merciless poison-tongued delinquent
Hiding the quiet man inside
To my dad's amazement
You grew up and flew away
Sharing your dreams
Leaving your nightmare screams in some therapist's waste
     bin
You reached out and embraced the world as it is
And it shot you.

What if When

What if when
My sanitary protection
Lost all sense of itself and
Unashamedly slid
Down my unsuspecting salwar leg
In a room full of respected guests
And landed on the freshly laundered floor,
I refused embarrassment

What if when
My mother spat
Contempt crawling on her tongue
Take your filth with you.
Rather than attending to what I estimated to be
Thousands of eyes teeming with
The urge to eradicate this evil revelation,
I refused embarrassment

What if I had walked unashamedly forward?
Contested the blue blood of social fabric
Tentatively picked up the offender
Laughed as I disposed it.
Stood Proud at life's quirks?
And refused embarrassment?

What if when
The first bleed that came from begrudged places
Did not burn but washed away childhood aches?
Was not an indication the almighty had rejected me?
Would I have skipped through the house?
In anticipation of the joys of adulthood

Rather than serving the sentence for
Eve's misdemeanours.

In place of the humiliation of the
Cycle of perpetual contamination
What if I refused embarrassment?

Vanessa Fay

Limbs

Lightness and levitation
knows her head space
as she cradles her stomach carrying dead pasts
hurtling, pining towards stillness
quiet inhalation

and she and I are at a train station
going to anywhere away from here
I pick at the skin around my finger nails
whilst her legs settle,
for a while silence flirts with us

sometimes, I think she's from another place, time,
        or kingdom
she smells of across the sea
she weeps algae
she moves with rippled tide
she speaks to me of being submerged

like looking up to the underbelly of a gull
or driving through winding trees
the dappled light proliferating, smattering the windows
a strobe-light disco

like realising you are misplaced
and that it is better that way.
she has February in her eyes
summer noontide bedraggling her tired frame

she is confused voices in the distance
metallic birdsong whilst trying to sleep
a collision between gravity and trying
she is exotic and a twenty pence cup of tea

together we sing the blues, Joni Mitchell,
we are the moon and cold hands
younger than the pebbles we collected
discovered in coat pockets, forgotten
parts of something we are when we allow ourselves

CAROLINE ENGLAND

Ego

I listen as you wrap
me in your smile
but I don't really hear.
A penny for them
I want to say, a coin
to climb inside, to
examine and explore,
to dig and delve, to
hold up to the light
and say what's this?
What does it mean?

You show me yours
and I'll show you mine.
But I know I'd renege
on the deal. I'm not
prepared to share the
murky depths of my
closest friend, that critical
cow, sometimes truthful,
rarely kind but always there,
protective, comforting,
supportive, righteous,
outraged and smug.

I suppose I am as you are
but I don't know that
for sure and so I'll keep
the coin and invest in
something that's a safer bet.

SUE STERN

A Woman in Black

A woman in black passes me by.
Only dark pupils gleam
through slits in her woven mask,
then I notice her shoes,
elegant, high, with tiny jewels at the toe.

I'm walking to Cheadle.
I think I should stop, say, 'Hello,
are you new? When did you come to live here?'
But she's gone.

If we could really speak, I would tell her this,
that my grandmother too was a stranger
in a strange land. How she fled Arctic Russia,
the Tsar, travelled a million miles
to find shelter in gentle London.

I would say, I'm a woman like you.
I hold a grieving friend in my arms,
kiss the bruised hand of a child,
make Apple Crumble from garden fruits;
that journey from stove to table, I've made
a thousand, thousand times.
Rise when someone is sick in the night,
weep with joy when my son takes a wife,
with desolation when my daughter dies.
And pray that we're safe from danger,
that we'll all be well.

These are the things I would like to say
to the woman in black as she passes by.
Next time, I'll smile.

MATT GOODFELLOW

The Inauguration of Barack Obama

William sits, perched on my knee
one sock on and one sock off.
He taps his foot – perpetual motion.
'Who is Bawack Obama?' he asks,
turning his head to look at me.
'It's Barrrrack Obama,' I say, rolling my Rs.
'He's the new President of America,
that big country we talked about.'
'America? Oh.'
He pauses to watch.
Two men walk down huge white steps
each bearing the burden of a different future.
'Is that Bawack Obama?' he asks.
'Yes,' I say. 'He's about to become the
most powerful man in the world –
when you're older I'll remind you that
we watched it together.'
The information is filtered,
processed by the mind of a 3½ year old.
'Is he more powerful than red Power Ranger?' he asks,
'Yes,' I say.
He turns back to the TV and thinks.
'Oh. He's not more powerful than
Spiderman though is he?'
I make a choice – our eyes meet
separated by 6 inches and 25 years.
'No,' I say,
'Not as powerful as Spiderman.'

John Siddique

Pygmalionism

Silence made from all the things we say.
The question, which makes (my body, my soul)
the one thing we most want to speak out loud is

in the town at night, in the bars,
at work, in the profound moments of love
– silence made from all the things we say.

The weight of the tongue muted against time,
unknowing (almost knowing)
the one thing we most want to speak out loud is

constant at the root of each thought,
the root of each root, the words of the body,
the silence made from all the things we say.

A pressure within the throat, or a cold clear
night when we consider the names of stars.
The one thing we most want to speak out loud is

never said, or if it is, it is not heard,
even if we are capable of forming it in black ink
on white paper, it pulls the stars apart.
The one thing we most want to say out loud is

MATTHEW CURRY

It's Thursday Morning and You Can See

It's Thursday morning and you can see
the old lady waiting for the fish man,
in purple leg-warmers, green coat, grey hair,
red gloves. And an old-style pram parked there –
small wheels chrome tubes and a blue cavity.
She's given it a fluorescent strip,
and there's a black bin bag inside. The kip-
pers and cod will go in it – no baby's lip
has trembled here for a long time. You can
wait if you like and watch the fish man,
in apron and trimmed beard sharpen his knife,
and gravely with a cheery smile cut fillets
for the wrinkled lady who hovers and chats,
then pushes a pramful of fish back to life.

Philip Burton

Trouble at Mill

*Britain's oldest chairmaker was H J Berry of
Chipping village, Lancashire.*

I don't know why it got under my skin
that trying too hard to brush off a strike
the boss came and painted my lathe bright pink.

I could have laughed but I made a stink
and told him to paint his own parlour like.
I don't know why it got under my skin –

tarting machines up's no mortal sin.
But I told him to jump on his bloody bike.
The boss came and painted my lathe bright pink

which shouldn't have flaming hurt, but it did.
I'm not your fellow traveller type.
I don't know why it got under my skin.

Maybe it's just that he didn't think
and 'stead of asking what was the gripe
the boss came and painted my lathe bright pink

where it used to shine like a brass eyepin.
I tossed his paintbrush in Parlick Pike.
I don't know why it got under my skin –
the boss came and painted my lathe bright pink.

Hurting Kind

Huddled around her pain she crosses
the rain-spattered darkness of the road.

Night flashes tug at her gaze,
but she does not look,
does not turn aside.

The swish of tyres on wet tarmac
follows her footsteps
as she makes her way out of the natural and
into the artificial.

The harsh lights cast
sharp-edged shadows beneath her.

At the counter, words are exchanged and
a chair is offered.

She longs to curl onto the seat,
tucking her legs under her.

She longs to cradle
the child of pain
in her belly.

She longs to howl.

Her name is called and
she carries her ache
into the examination room.

As she crosses the threshold
she does not wonder

what will happen next.
She is beyond that.

All she longs for is an end.

SONIA TRÉPANIER

Because I Love this Land

Spitting at my heart. Raining on my town. Inundating
  my life.
Dressed as cats for no reason.
Where the kids flew,
Through the bench of illusions,
Dusk and dawn wish the poor lust for everyone.
House and glares,
Shining rugs,
Dark windows,
Obsolete beliefs.
Yes. I do
I do think of it.
Temporarily faded.
Hope and liquid.
Full of you.
Juggling tensions in between bracelets I bought for myself.
In between songs I learned.
Dreams I lost.
Or changed.
Or never had.
Three at the time.
Forever green.
Photographs and lines and drawings and prints of a past
  you'd wish.
The sun will rise.
It will be a fucking brand new day.

Lights in the Harbour

After the Alcohol Treatment Unit Relatives Meetings
we'd dash to The Albert, order a pint and a gin & tonic
to prove to ourselves we were ok, we could have just
the one and walk away relaxed, made more sociable.
We didn't have to pretend that morning gin was water,
or that the vodka bottle in the bin, under the pillow,
behind the bookcase was nothing to do with us, neither
of us desperate to stop shaking or remembering.
Unlike our relatives who'd been downstairs at AA
who were binge drinkers, drip-drinkers staying topped-up
all day and most of the night. Relatives who hid bottles
in cisterns, filled hoses in their garages with cheap whisky,
threw empty miniatures and flat bottles into neighbours'
gardens, knew the exact time the offy opened and had
pockets big enough to stash vodka all the way home.

Another? you say. No thanks, I say, watching the man
on his own order two pints for last orders, carry them
back to his table in the corner, fumble out a coin and put
Sea of Heartbreak on the juke box.

CARLY HIND

The Comings and the Goings

for all of our comings and goings
we   come and we   go.
ladyandchild whisper
    words,
    wishes
or maddening secrets that
stumble
and
slip

out of bloodying mouths in a
drip dripdrip.

MAX WALLIS

Modern Love: Texting

We send each other text messages at work.
Discuss what we're having for lunch.
Ether-joined by unlimited messages and pixel screens.
Two minutes after saying goodbye on dates
our phones jangle, vibrate,
'I had a lovely time tonight :-)'

The little xx means more from you.
You give me fewer than my mum.
I look and linger at them, there,
at the end of your miniature letters.
Save the sweet ones in a folder
and read them when down.

'These are the reasons I love you.'
'Do you want to go to the cinema at four?'
'I've never felt this before.'
I smile when I see your name appear.

The lump is a plastic pebble in my pocket
heavy with the weight of expectancy.
Linked to everything, almost sentient
it throbs with the lives
of so many people a button press away:
Facebook, e-mails, Google
and you.

When people are gone: vanished.
Ephemeral ghosts that exist
but don't. That breathe,
but don't.

The wishing wells in which we shed our coins.
Our thumbs linger over "DELETE"
as though they'll disappear from memory, too.

Punch. Gone. The love letter's dead.
Think that'll make us feel better.
When our hearts turn red again,
we'll wish we had the numbers still
to say
hello, hi, how do you do.

Cat Watching

A wondrous cat,
a silky cat,
sharpening claws
on a coconut mat.
Neat little fangs
as white as snow,
whiskers long
as whiskers grow.

Leaping, looping,
arched and flat.
Hissing, spitting,
jaws that chat.
Green eyes flow
to gold and black,
silent paws on verdant track.

This smoky cat
with shards of white,
abroad by day
and moonless night.
Savage lands lie in her eyes,
whilst hunting mice and butterflies.

All these things and so much more,
wispy ears and pink-pad paw,
coaxing purrs and wafting tail,
soft allures that rarely fail.

Languorous, sinew'd, stretched and still,
basking on a window sill,
sun-warmed, smiling, breathing deep,
fierceness quelled whilst fast asleep.

Throughout her days of shades and bowers,
no ownership can make her ours,
her loyalty is hers to give,
where to stay and where to live.
Open doors that hold no sway,
her choice to go, her choice to stay.

Nicolas Costello

Kestrel Super

This is West– wood, zero trees an' all squares limps an'
      tarmac
Snares, a slick rained daft o'clock car light split the block in
      pairs of
Ecstatic

This is West– wood, an' round here the moon did an
      abashed sway
Soft half– pinned an' lidded

I'd been to see music, seen a princess of drum an' cymbal
      sing blond
Perfect from a trolley, seen some twat screamin' love in my
      ear

Black hair an' slim hip lifted in majors an' minors, music for
      the stars
For beggars an' choirs

Different from the West-wood, from the terraced unkempt
      the dreams
Left undreamt, from the red boudoir bunk-bed sisters the
      mothers
With blisters movin' on a dozen tip-toes past ABCs in the
      night, no
Sleep, just a damp shut- eyed slowness on this street

Step-like shook with four Stellas, slow licked down the
      pavement an'
Two fellas stood before a van, blue transit bravado, the
      bonnet
Cocked to the night

Silent mechanics, I thought, see how their tools do not even
     rattle like
Cutlery but wrench the air spotless

My step-like quick an' broke the evenin' in a blast of tin-lilt
     can silence
An' thin-wilt divan caress, I did not see them at first

Perhaps two or three shapes that swirled black romantic an'
     peerless
Where no pristine eye-lash clearness is, lay upon tartan and
     prob'ly
On nan's old settee collapsed in the backin' his white thighs
     strongly
Slappin' up against her doze
...

This is the West– wood, the land of the swaggerin' ode, of
     the piss–
Stained penguins of old Percy an' Keats who sit writin' in
     needle
Parks not of nightingales or skylarks, but of a pinioned
     kestrel love,
Unknown locks, clearer frowns an' slurred fuck offs
...

A place of unlikely rakes all trundling bones and unlikelier
     odes under the
Blushing moon.

GORDON ZOLA

The Name Game

Is life a battle,
if you come from Hastings?
If you come from Chorley,
is it a piece of cake?
Do you have to be a tart
to live in Bakewell?
And if your name's Sleep,
are you ever awake?

Do you deserve applause
if you come from Clapham?
Do you never shower
if you come from Bath?
Are you more than a ham
if you come from Sandwich?
And if your name's Giggles
are you game for a laugh?

Do Smiths forge for a living?
Are Meeks humble and giving?
Are Dances having a ball?
And if your name's Foot,
are you twelve inches tall?

If you come from Avon,
are you always calling?
If you're an Angel
are you always falling?
Are Wrights ever wrong?
If your name's Singh
Do you know the song?

If you come from Leeds
do you never follow?
If your name's Joy
Have you known no sorrow?
If it's Cain, are you never Able?

Or, are we much more than a label?
Do we have to keep playing the name game?
Repeating the same again and again.
Playing out life's dramas,
with all its panoramas.

Hopping on and off the carousel.
Trying to salvage heaven,
From someone else's hell.

Coz when that last penny and breath are spent,
and it's time to take that final curtain call.
What we're called, or where we come from,
Will mean… FUCK ALL.

DAVE VINEY

Hobson's Choice Words

Noisy neighbours,
this is your time!

Go forth and multiply the beat,
with 50-inch sub-woofers and tweeters –
Masterbeaters of the highest order,
revel in your disorder.

Give us this day our daily bass
and forgive us our wall-hangings,
as we forgive those who wall-bang against us.

Noisy neighbours,
this is your moment!

Assemble your fellow scrotes and vote chaos.

Save us from temptation to sleep
and deliver us from peaceful,
with karaoke / off-key.

But know this...
Our time is coming

and you will not hear us coming,
'cause we are bleary-eyed black belts in consideration,
a tip-toenado, a subtle shift in power
and we're raising glass after glass,
hour upon hour

to Payback!

To bittersweet revenge,
to turning speakers up against the wall at 6am,

with the way-too-loud, dulcet tones of Radio 4 –
like fingernails on blackboards,
to the muppets next door.

To the look that says
'If I don't sleep tonight,
you might just sleep forever,'
to domestics drowned out
by the great British weather,
to the blown fuses, the refuges
and the six week cruises,
to decent breeding, silent reading
and legal proceedings.

We do not wish you dead, although
the irony would not be wasted on us,
if you overdosed on sleeping pills,
or got hit by a truck transporting earplugs.

We'll leave you with this...
Five minutes of peace.
Five whole minutes of peace.

But we'll lace every second,
with the threat of noise
and share a private joke
at your glimmer of hope,
when we offer you Hobson's Choice.

Liz Loxley

Flesh

Money talks in the meat market;

but, if meat itself could talk,
its voice would have
the same metallic tang
as coins or blood;

a voice from deep inside a vein
pumped at the tender
crook of arm; skin,
thin as notes passed from
hand to hand, again and again
and again.

Men with eyes wide as an ox's
glide in metal, idle at kerbsides;
sniff the glisten and drip of it.

I feel such tenderness for meat.

REBECCA AUDRA SMITH

Mummy Gazing at Manchester Museum

Shallow graves in the sand,
Dip your finger and brush bones
The wind warps a desert,
Pulls back the veil of dust, of burial
Shows new eyes old bodies…

Still human, still the skeleton you feel
When you press your hands to your lover's back
The fine tuning of their fingers rubs your ribcage
Delves, burrows to get to your lungs, your liver,
Your stomach, and box them up neat.
You might need them later.

They would hook your brain out from your nose
Like a sneeze, and dissolve the rest with chemicals
Like a crime, solving the puzzle of what the dead do
With their spare time, they pick themselves up,
Re-root their eyes, their heart intact in their hollow chests,

Cheating death. Our world is charted by clocks yet
I'm a step away from these tombs.
"Behold, you are young again forever,"
Chants bring them back, the glass
That separates me from a corpse decays,
Becomes its elements: sand, sand, the heat of our sun.

Richard C Mather

Exodus 20:21

"Moses approached the thick darkness where God was."
— Exodus 20:21

God is the black chasm
at the heart of the cosmos,
or to think of it another way,
the snuffing out of life
on the edge of creation.

We usually think of God as
light but I think of
God as *darkness*,
a profound,
glittering *darkness*,
an abyss of Being,
from where
creation is expelled
and one day
must return.

We talk about God as
presence but I think about
God as
absence, a God
whose best miracle is to
vanish and go
into hiding
either in the middle of things
or way out on the brink.

He is a secreted God
who, when
you find him

at the edge of space
or in the depths of
the polar ice caps,
or sheltered under a tree
in the driving rain,
conceals you beneath his
thick black cape.

Or enfolds you in his
enormous brooding wings,
(black as crow feathers);
or purges you to a cinder
in the burning foliage
of his undying love;
or lays you to rest
at the centre
of a supernova

just before it explodes.

MARY BRETT

Nurturing Night

In an old cottage, roofed with thatch,
she dreams beneath the moon.
A long-haired blonde, in ruffled white,
seventeen that June.
And as she dreams, night brings escape,
from scholarly irons, and competitive hate,
for energies stir, through all in that place,
drifting through curtains of lace.

(drifting through curtains,
drifting through curtains,
drifting through curtains, of lace.)

Mists are swirling in the marsh,
close by the garden gate.
A black cat steps down an old oak tree,
to the faerie wench who waits.
An owl is hooting, and past the moon,
three bats now hover, a weird triune,
and winds do roam, and rustle the grass,
down to where few footsteps pass.

(down to where few footsteps,
down to where few footsteps,
down to where few footsteps pass.)

A clear call has been made;
subconsciously, responsively;
and from its grave, glides a shade,
to the maid's bedside, by sympathy swayed...

Fragments linger, in her mind,
as daybreak tints the fields.

Dressing, weary, sad, alone,
to discipline she yields.
But all that day, she'll know the face,
the quaint-toned voice, and the languid grace,
of one, she thinks, was only a dream,
born upon a moonbeam.
Born, upon a moonbeam.

In Requiem

On the purpled-ribboned
Black-tie limousine morning
Relatives speak
In sherry tainted breath
How best to divide
The spoils of death
Sisters and daughters
In funeral frocks
Argue over carriage clocks
And who holds the keys
To mother's box
Sons-in-law sit
Stone-faced in pairs
And squabble over stocks and shares
Regency dressers
Queen Anne chairs
What is and is not theirs
Throughout the morning
Nephew and nieces
Takeaway small bits and pieces
Nervous fingers twirl on cigarettes
As at the cemetery gates
The stage is set
For tears at the grave
And false regrets

Raymond

Surprised he goes to auctions, buys antiques
'But why?' I asked. Turning towards my voice,
'Well, porcelain is beautifully smooth
but not, admittedly, my favourite choice.'
His hands, dancing in air, formed lovely curves.
'I do give in at times to the temptation;
rely on others to describe the piece,
knowing I miss the painted decoration.
Cut glass, now, that's the best.' Hand movements jerked,
hinted at diamonds, squares. 'Fine workmanship,
so intricate, precise, is such a joy.
I feel the flaws, too, never make a slip.
Glass, as I'm well aware, is colourless;
my fingers give me the advantage there.
"We missed that chip," they sometimes say. I gloat.
"Well, just admit, friends, that is only fair." '
His hands spread wide to emphasize his joke.
I marvelled at their skill, eager to find
their own illumination, which creates
detailed, non shining patterns in his mind.

Simon Rennie

The Outgrowing

1.

Where did the greenhouse go?

For years it stood
rooted in concrete
on the nursery grounds,
trapping the heat from
weak sun and strong,
mothering feeble seedlings
with life-bringing light
and the milk of moisture.

Eager green shoots
stood row upon row
in their cups of earth,
their sterile environs
and off-kilter seasons,
waiting for the approval
of continued care,
or the brusque discarding
that inevitably follows
the recognition of defects.

And those that remained
strengthened their stems
and grew up and out,
wanting only to touch
the glass that sheltered them,
to caress the steel frame
that constructed their world.

2.

When the business went bust
the nursery was abandoned;
waterless soil caked and cracked
and many plants perished.
The survivors bolted, panicked,
now sought the glass with vengeance,
pushing at the panes until they broke,
fell, shattered unheard
on the greenhouse floor.

For the first time the plants
felt real rain, real weather.
In their anger they danced mad
in the wind, guzzled the sun.
With their now woody branches
they forced and distorted
the corroded empty frames
until they buckled, rusty rivets popping.
The structure creaked and toppled,
pulling the twined plants with it
to the wild ground beneath.

Their anger spent, the plants died,
rotted, fed the earth for weeds to grow;
weeds with no carers but Chance and Nature.
The steel frames melted to ferrous rivulets,
little orange waters, mineral constituents.
The stony soil sucked down the broken glass,
breaking it further and rounding its edges.
Time rolled out its mindless unmaking.

That is where the greenhouse went.

Friedrich Karl

Friedrich Karl takes a cafetière to Sainsbury's
(there's a snack bar inside, but he scoffs at convention)
and drinks from a mug as he walks past the shelves,
hooking a right at the end of the row
(where jars of red beetroot that resemble his parents
are two for a pound) to stroll past the bakery
and fire a cool gaze down the aisle's enfilade.
Male Grooming, Home Baking and Asian Cuisine
are offered for sale. None appeal to Friedrich.
Nor do the boxes of cereals scattered
(along with a trolley, its wheels askew)
across his path in aisle thirteen.
Their packets boast loudly of fortified whole grains
in language which seems to our hero unspeakably
flat. Riboflavin and B12 are not
what he's seeking. His head's full of Huysmans and other
dangerous long-deceased writers. He sighs
at Best Ever, and New and Improved:
these words are so functional, lazy, prosaic.
For nine months he's worked as a sign copywriter:
it's his job to make sure the public don't go through
the wrong door, slip on a slippery floor,
overlook high-tension lines, drown at sea,
take a dog where a dog should never be taken.
It's getting him down. No Public Access.

Accepting convention, Friedrich Karl
leaves by the doors marked Exit, but now
he's a goal. Over nine months the world had become
more pedantic, less magical, because he had written these
     signs.

For nine months he'd worked at a job that he hated,
but the time was not wasted. Nine months he'd gestated
the plan that now burst forth to the front of his mind.
Cheap stolen coffee and raw desperation
gave birth to his vision: he'd rewrite poetically
all the signs he found dull, make their words bright and new.
If he failed, no problem: he'd comfort himself
with a chocolate flapjack and a mug of warm hemlock.

Back in his flat, where bowls of uneaten
cold gleimous porridge were scattered across
his sofa and floor, Friedrich Karl struck a pose
and waited for rare inspiration to strike.
How to attract Muses? Are they brought near
by candles, soft lighting? He'll do without them.
Straining for words with the labour of Heracles
(he thinks to himself that evoking the Greeks
can't do any harm) he opens his mouth
and slowly says:
        O!
It seems a good start.
Settling back for a minute to rest
he looks for a pen. Don't want to forget this.
But his neocortex is firing anew.
        O Cervine Egress!
He pauses. That doesn't
seem bad for a sign warning drivers of deer.
He scribbles it down on the back of his hand.
Within half an hour he's written four more
and his ambition's soared to iambic pentameter:
        Traveller, beware! for on this road
        play children, frolicking and gamb'lling in
        your path. Erected hereupon are raiséd
        mounds, to slow your way. For years beyond
        all memory's span, since days unknown they have
        been here, your safety consciousness to prove.
        The course of Crewe Road never did run smooth.

How preferable, this, to a sign reading Humps!
If people should need to slow down lest they not
see the words, the road would be made all the safer.
And so he is ready, gathers sandpaper, pens,
a bottle of bleach and a box of teabags
(why he's got this last he isn't quite clear,
but you can't be too sure, and he's taking no chances),
and sets out the door. He'll scrub off the old
and write on the new. Farewell to his guilt.

But as he goes searching for a Men at Work sign,
        Expect Delays Till September '11
(which he wants to replace with
        Man labours in vain
        as the earth turns – twice shall the moon
        turn upon itself before the work's done)
the signs start to hit back. Simply at first:
        Snow Drifts
– nature poetry. As the wind blows and rain falls,
Friedrich Karl reflects briefly on the truth of these words.
Then come calls to arms:
        Blind Children
(Friedrich wonders
if he's missed his calling) and tales of lost love:
        Stop If Directed
        Keep Your Distance
        Await Rescue
And Friedrich Karl thinks of Margaret who left him
for a shambling, itinerant, colporteur from Ayr
        (Changed Priorities Ahead)
She said he was childish,
a dreamer, not realistic. She poured scorn
on plans to establish a chain of poetic plumbers
who'd suck through their teeth at your newly-sprung leak
and assert that the water ruining the ceiling
resembled your eyes, deep pools in the wilds
of your face, and he'd order some parts but didn't

know when they'd arrive and besides this model's
gone out of production, and the dark patch on your wall
that grew by the minute mapped out your destiny,
see, here where these two veins of life-giving aqua
meet, that's where we'll finally touch lips, one another,
and the call-out's ten pounds, plus VAT,
I'll see you next Thursday. It's the best I can do.
Margaret hated this idea that he cherished,
but she was beautiful. Friedrich Karl won't do better.

Without knowing how, he's walked across the city
lost in his thicket of regretful thoughts,
and finds himself ambling down the M62,
his feet grazing the grass by the highway's hard shoulder.
His sandpaper's rubbed a hole right through his jacket,
the pens lost to nature, the bleach leaked away.
He sits on a barrier and looks at a sign
which urges him on while holding him back.
  No Stopping. No U-Turns.
The traffic roars by
and Friedrich Karl wonders where the white patch
on his shirt could have come from. The sign fades from view
as the sun sinks behind a broken-down lorry,
its wheels askew. On his chosen path,
FK takes a teabag from a trouser pocket.
Gazing at the tarmac, he silently sucks.

STEVE WALSH

The Run in Blue Hill

low moor
broad wood
ivory february field
iron tan hard
frost cracked
shard-eared earth's
crust ice
pistol plosive

pewterslate sky,
dun, green edged
gentle hill, grass
glass sharp

hare's bend carves
slice curved
blue air
wind and rain
wild water flowing
rhythm and wave

a sombre drumbeat
pulse
percussion pump
powering limbs

ears clang
breaths clamour
blood cells song
howl heart's hammer

soft spray
scents of oil green
mystic jewels of leaf
mingle
crisp, white, gold
a fine mist of cells
atoms brainblow
a rainbow

LYNN WALTON

Sleepless Beauty

restless dance floor
shuffles its offerings

he coils closer
to reap one

her girl-smile drowned in lipstick
body in retreating clothes

in the crawling darkness
of a black-seamed back street
he smudges her
against a greasy wall

indifferent streetlights
elsewhere pavements
distracted buildings

girls sprinkle tell-me eyes
on their unravelled friend

clotted words
scratch at
thorns across
her mouth

Neil McCall

Cocks and Horses

I mount the grinning skewered stallion,
you grasp the saddled bird to my inside,
gold and scarlet as
an Indian bride.

Salt spray and onions in the autumn air,
hit-chart calliope whirls us higher
into the gaudy heart
of Lancashire.

I rise and you fall; I fall and you rise,
your hair a wild mane tossed in tungsten light
kiss me quick as trams
in the rainy night.

Dizzy and puddled we stagger to bed
till bacon beckons and herring gulls call
the cocks and horses
the child in us all.

K M Hallenberg

Ain't No Love in Here, Girl

whatcha come in here for, girl? whatcha come in here for?
ain't no love in here, ain't no love, girl. it's all gold-strewn
gutters in here, age-old lies and cold-hearted fuckers. and
when they smile, it hurts like a blind-bitch, like a wrench to
the face. whatcha want that for, girl?

well ain't it grand, girl? ain't it grand? this water-clogged,
down-trodden city of blood-diamonds? full of blood-hounds
and dead baby-foxes and us, girl. knee-deep in bodies and
it's grand. fuck, but it's grand.

you won't win, girl. you won't win. you'll get a card-tower, a
case-file, a victim-number of your very own, girl. and them
coppers, them guards of vice and virtue, they'll stand over
you with their hard-as-nails-seen-it-all-eyes. so you
remember that, girl. you won't win. the house always does.

better run, girl. better run past the mile-markers and the
money-makers, the movers and the shakers. they've got no
love, girl, not like ours. so you run girl. you run and take that
creed-given, free-falling love, like lanes of morning traffic,
like kites in the sky. run fast, girl. run fast. i'm right behind
you.

Valium Skies

Valium skies surround the fulcrum,
Open hands, as diving gulls, circling in flight.
Voices surround me, echoes offering guidance,
Sirens sounding, escaping promise,
Lost in silence and fallen voices.

Settled into a state of permanent loss,
Saint Elizabeth's, steel blade, dripping potions.
Keys without function and bound in slumber,
A timber shell creaks and groans under, as
The narrative falls apart. The mind wanders.

Scratched words and symbols merge and waver,
Our souls scream in distilled sadness.
Drugs to savour and cured of malady,
My imagination in patterns, formed in normality,
Cerebral reality reverted to factory settings.

Original experiences fade in a glazy doom,
Distant sepia strives to hold them back.
Even dreams of screaming horses.
The fulcrum now disturbed, branched off fighting wars,
Aligned in perfect symmetry.

Candle-soft memories eclipse jarring dreams,
Dancing syllabubs lie bereft, calm. Serene.
I learn to breathe in shallow thoughts, still,
Endless fires darkly chilled, surround the gold ochre.
Writing now within freedom as past lives disperse.

Allowed to wander in those forgotten seas,
Shrouds of my past, in shallow forms sleep.

My pages at last torn free from binding,
A mind ripped clear from dark confused clarity.
History stretched over cracked vellum scripts.

Freedom is glimpsed in this spectrum, kept thin,
The fox no longer runs from the farmer.
The hens within, from their fixed cages knowing,
Openings in a wall broke free from structure.
Showing a place thought lost. Unspoken.

Gentle rainbows bow in sight,
Bright symphonies now charged with promise.
The eyes of this shell crackle still, dousing rain.
Visions glide on the boat, tethered no more,
Drifting hope merged into light crimson skies.

Xmas Kisses

tonite tonite
the party's on.
boys in white shirts,
girls flashing their thongs.
tonite, the rules were meant to bend.

ladies & gentlemen:
step right up! take yr pick!
christmas kisses fallin fast.
catch em, fellers
& tonite u might dip yr wick.

cos these streets are stained with lipstick.
the walls are drippin,
saliva's alive & thick.
no need to wipe yr chin or ask yr mates,
'does my breath smell of sick?'
who cares,
when the kisses are fallin so quick?

they come in all shapes & sizes:
some tongueless booby prizes,
some wetlipped & mushy, all slobberin & slushy,
some rushed & mistaken identities,
'wait, wait!
eww, i thought u were yr mate!'

there's a blizzard of kisses.
there's hits & near misses that stick to the air
& abandon their fate.
some are blushing & tender,
or rough like weekends on a bender.

then, there's those that are desperate to get some tongue
action, before it strikes two & it's all too late.

kisses for me
save all yr kisses for me

& there's
kisses & kisses
like a swarm of wet bees,
like plunging winter holidays in the south seas divin so deep
yr tongue's like jonah in the whale comin up for air faces
spinnin red & white disco lights singin here it is merry
christmas! all yr crew shoulder to shoulder couldn't give a
monkeys...
stagger to the bar beer splashin cleavages & bare legs
promisin a warm bed. tonite's the night when months of
fantasies take flight.

now, the dj spins the classic tunes begin:

... guilty feet have got no rhythm

"careless whisper" drags u to the dancefloor, grindin hips,
sticky fingers, sweaty lips, hands that linger half-heartedly
slapped, as two o'clock strikes, the brutal lights reveal
couples half undressed under tables slowly uncouple, queue
for coats, stumble down the stairs, crackin dirty jokes into
piccadilly plaza, the busies all busy tryin to start a fight, u
dodge the flyin bottles, pissin in an alley way, wait for a taxi,
shiverin in a long line of pimpled pink & white shirts stained
with blood & somebody else's drink,

as the bloke from finance pulls up in a jag,
the bird u thought u had gets in & leaves u shouting,
'bitch, i knew u was a slag!',
& a sudden twitch sends sixteen pints of triple x & four
southern comforts out yr nose.

u wake up
arms wrapped
tight
around
a white
cold
toilet bowl.

Moving In

there's a picture of a corner shop printed
on the tiles in the kitchen, boasting linen and
fresh produce from centuries ago. i sweep
coffee granules from the counter, lift twin
steaming cups to the bedroom. the floorboards
creak and groan. all my stuff's laid out; clothes
piled in a new wardrobe, big enough to hide in.
curtains and bed sheets clash like dogs and cats.

i said goodbye but kept my keys. like i was never
really leaving, made plans for curry and cocktails
so i could still be that ghost. floating from room to
room and calling each one home. anonymity at large.
i've a list of broken postcodes on my phone
reminding me where to go. each door is left ajar.

sticky limbed and silent at 2am, i sweep the covers
from my shoulders. we try to sleep, in this strange
hotel hell with someone else's heating bill. empty
mugs and boxes have piled up. there's a special
spot for baggage in a house where people speak too
loud. i'll cry about it when the lights are out, but
tomorrow – we'll explore this town.

JOEY CONNOLLY

Loss

What is it – reassurance? – I get
from the thought of obscure & complicated
numerical transactions occurring
in sad, former-soviet towns, in
cold, dusty, Eastern-European towns ringed
with collapsing fences, in post offices or
private rooms, with balance books
& iron-looking machines with
sliding parts & till rolls or ribbons
& outdated conversion tables
to rely on, unlaminated & hopeless?
And why? To know that tiny, tangle-fine flares
of complication are going up, everywhere
and always; that light
could trickle through the uppermost leaves
of raspberry canes, say, and find
so many angles of surface, so many surfaces
to angle on? That we, too,
might be the same, with our words,
our figures, our rituals and calculations
& lookings-up? That everything has its catch,
and nothing at all is slipping past too easily?

Train Journey One

Welcome aboard the 20:51 Alcohol Express service to
        Hangover Central
We will be stopping at:
A Few Quiet Drinks
One More Pint
Free Shot Bar
Bad Dance Park
Pissed Parade
Kebab North
Cab Home Street
Sick Green
Collapse Stream
Weird Dream
Hangover-Upon-Soar
And Hangover Central

Please change at One More Pint
To access the availability
Of services to Boredom or Sensibility

The buffet car will open shortly
With an array of overpriced snacks
So sit back, relax
And keep telling yourself that you will enjoy the journey

Am Sad

Am sad
am to pluck hair out
am to grip onto my skin
and hold it tight
am to think everything except the kitchen sink
am to be aware of fragile faith
am clutch it tight
onto the same felt
the same stealth
hand be: touching gland
and touché:
    am sad
am to not feel good
rocky heart
temperous mentality
use of no: purpose
dead end, no shifts
no work
no wage
no name
no place
sick emotion when thinking where home is
as sad, is where the heart is

JOLEEN LEWIS

F**k the BNP

I am British
yeah me
though probably
and strongly disagreed
by the BNP.

'Cause when they look at me
and see
the tightly curled hair
the thickly formed lips
the chocolate coloured skin that I am in

they will say...
'She's not British.'

But! I talk with an accent
unlike some others
I say shit like,
'Ya wat' and 'Safe'
just like my sisters and brothers.

But when I say I'm British some dickheads disagree
and say...
'Nar Love, you're just 5.2 percent of the ethnic minority.'

It's not that I am not proud of my beautiful history and roots
I mean I love my people
my culture
the music and the fruits...
But I Am British!
I support British teams,
I mean as a teen standing on the pitch at Anfield was one of
        my dreams.

Though I'm not a fan of your queen
I'm not a Brit to that extreme
I'm not keen on the whole regime and
I don't get your love for tea...
But I Am British!

I was taught in three British schools
I abide by British rules
Yeah, I grew up on soul and reggae
but
I think Kate Bush and Coldplay are cool.

I was there
through Thatcher, Major and Blair (and the other two)
Throughout the IRA bomb scares
Felt my house shake when they hit town and brought
        Manchester down!

But yet!
They force me to tick that box
Which I think's a disgrace!
What have my office typing skills got to do with my fucking
        race?

But isn't it obvious?
Look at my face.
But what you get is what you see.

So FUCK the BNP
'Cause I'm British,
yeah me.

ANNETTE COOKSON

Manchestarr

Cars bikes buses trams
to a Market Street
that's always rammed
with buskers, hustlers
and mums pushing prams.
Down come the high rise
lives of the hinterlands,
up go apartments
that specialise, compartmentalise.
Spatial division
for the masses, still
that fine line
between the classes.
Public gardens
fountains, pop queens emos chavs
and drunks, music
sung live from praise God
to funk as bubbles blow
Mancunian dreams
over the head of Victoria.
Pavements are canvas
full of rainbows and poets,
Monet prints of
surreal chewing gum
come into focus
and play with
the light in your eye.
With pride in the heart
and arrogance worn on feet
I walk these streets, these roads
with a smile and a swagger

through every nook and cranny in
its glorious crown
koz this is my Manc'land,
my muse,
my town.

Angela Topping

Presbytery Housekeeper

"How happy are the poor in spirit,
theirs is the kingdom of Heaven."
— Matthew's Gospel

The polish elbow-greased till he could see his face,
was all the love she dared betray.
Her laundered linen rounded on the line;
starched and ironed, it glorified the altar.
His noticing would make her sing
as she sat buffing up brass candlesticks
to a fitting shine, by blackening her hands.
The letterbox was quotidian –
its brass mouth opened to important letters
she conveyed to his desk with reverence.

Scrubbing the tiled floor was silent prayer.
The worn brush softened as she wrote his name in soap.
Her rejoicing over finding a choice cut of lamb,
affordable for his Sunday treat, outdid Heaven's.
She made cups of tea, asked him about his day
and listened. He never knew how one short word,
a harsh tone unheard in his own head,
could make her reproach herself all night.
She'd kneel in confession once a week,
'Father forgive me for all my sins'.

STUART A PATERSON

Justin

Justin has sunk his teeth in my arm
for the third time today, and I'm wistfully thinking
of dental prints, evidence, conviction
while I prise his gin-trap gob away.
This boy wears freckles like some exotic
Lepidoptera sport eyespots,
has a mouth that opens forever crammed
with terraces of tooth.
Rumpelstiltskin in Reeboks brays
a treasured soubriquet in my face,
Scotty Boy!, before retreating to his
room, his bed, a wholly darker place.
Shortly after, Eminem's *Without Me*
starts up in time to the frightening growls
of a metamorphosing banshee.
Memory-checking my boosters are
up to date, I fetch some Savlon and a plaster,
go upstairs, place a chair outside his door,
sit like post-divorce Rapunzel, wait.

CHARLOTTE GRINGRAS

Libeskind's War Memorial North
The Eagle Has Landed

Curving, dipping, it swoops and dives
in ways that buildings usually don't:
solidly Northern, it's an outsize kite,
a predatory bird, ready for the kill.
Visible rivets hold vast, gun-metal
sheets, glinting as sunlight streaks
over them – yes, here in Salford
something gleams!
Under the arches, matt-black
pebbledash mimics weaponry inside,
the canal, oily-dark, licks its base.
Massive, monumental, it dwarfs houses,
lorries, cranes; paints Lowry people
in miniature – Salford, flattened
by a war memorial.

MANTZ YORKE

Tyrant

On the box, Idi Amin's expansive smile hid
a brutality we found difficult to reconcile
even when we knew. Like him, you
are a paradox. The vicarage bonhomie

you use when you want to impress
flips when things don't go your way
to an intemperate trumpeting
that heads will roll. You're clever, of course,

in your self-centredness: you'd never
have made it without your network
of influence and your narrow-eyed calculus
of advantage. But deep down you fear

your father's ghost, and are threatened
by those who differ – a weak king protected
by a carapace of scars, surrounding yourself
with courtiers who daren't dissent.

That makes you dangerous. You bring
a Dalek's sentencing to opposition –
"Exterminate." Before the Roman nobility
can organise its disenchantment

you turn its members into corpses, unrevivable
at the play's end. Others, thrown out of time,
survive amongst ferns and horsetails,
knowing that one day they'll smell

the foetor of your breath and suffer
the tearing of talons and teeth.

Way back, did you listen in your classroom
to How Things Began? And can you remember

two children and their uncle crouching
in the undergrowth, watching a monstrous beast
with warty skin and dagger-like claws
stalk a gentle herbivore; the strike;

the slashing of claws and teeth; the screams
from the brackish ooze? If you can,
you'll also remember how things ended:
the beast with dagger-like claws... Dead.

The Willy Wonka Death Camp

He was a porn flake, a cereal thriller,
a toasty darkness warm and spluttery on the tongue.
Yeah! That Jesus bread sure tasted like salt and leper
to this atheist's soul buds. Bring it on godless god,
our thirst for life is the equal of your thirst for death.

He was a no man from the land of yes, under his breath
he fake danced and body sopped, avoiding the daily tongue
lashing of authority, the sun-dead side of town his fiefdom,
the apathy bomb left him radiant inactive, scared for life of
    truth,
where he now stays, a hidden amendment to the bill of
    shites.

He was a working talking sleeping stalking living dying
    voodoo doll,
worshipping the fascism of happiness, the fatal politics of
    party times,
dripping in passions of crime and the sob, sob, sob of so
    many sorrys,
he broke the heart's bank, flooded the mother lode, tried to
    father
a new Earth, one where he could touch something that
    didn't hurt.

The answer my friend is not blowing off to see the wizard
    not to follow the
yellow brick road to the Willy Wonka death camp of
    dissident Oompa-Loompas,
maybe it's time to turn off obeying and tune in to the world's
    emergency call
before you become just another tin lion munching on a
    straw-hearted world.

The Moon

The moon was watching me tonight.
At first I looked back, raising an eyebrow.
No response.

I tried a different approach.
Face relaxed, strolling,
I faked ignorance.

I could feel its glare.

A couple passed by
on the other side of the road,
pretended not to notice.

I decided to confront the situation.
My pace quickened.
I raised my chin and stared.
This seemed to work,
it hid behind the branches of a Wych Elm.
Then reappeared,
peeking at first,
then fully, boldly.

Beaten at my own game I turned away, blushing.
Smiling to myself, flattered.
'Why me?'

I gave a sideways glance and a flick of my lashes.
Light stroked my skin.

My head rolled, eyes shut.
It kissed me gently on the neck.

I reached my door.
Once inside, safe, I leaned back against the wood.
'Same time tomorrow.'

Peter J Viggers

Still Life

At night writing poems, ignoring sleep.
The gas fire's low, the armchair warm,
your bed is cold. Concerned with metre
and rhyme you don't want one dead
word in the middle of your illness.
Your clock neglects to measure time.

P A Livsey

Asleep

A child sleeps in body-warm
blankets, cosy, enveloped in
unreality as moonlight
plays in and out of shadows.

February's frost, glistening to the
moon's tune, froze windows shut,
icy-toothed taste of dawning
drifted in biting, biting relentlessly.

The child disarranges as dreams
unfold into vividness, not nightmarish.
Outside below the frost line insects
sleep, entrenched in subterranea.

Hedgehogs hidden and hibernating,
locked in winter's crystal cages
oblivious to a fox skulking, sniffing,
listening and pawing for a meal.

Frozen ground, frozen sound
bumps turn into glaciers for the errant
their body cold under a frost load.
No rug-snug bug here.

Trapped beneath an icy sheet
awaiting tomorrow's thawing
nature's natural clock shaping,
shades of night new life, new dreams.

The child stirs, stretches, yawns
confused into reality,
seeking the warmth of covers
fingers counting the cold's cost.

Darren Thomas

The Wood

They lay between
the shadowed cheeks of two trees
within the green blankets of its ferns
purple buttons of its flowers
and they stared
at the stillness in one another
inhaling the scents from a single June Saturday
hours inside a bowl of memories
gathered from a gorgeous, gorgeous wood.

The two trees stood either side of a man and a woman
four hundred years of knowing in their leaves
and they whispered to the silent people
'you know they will cherish one another'
and the flowers
through mouths perfumed with colour
chatted with dashes of dragonflies
who all appeared to have agreed
'they have begun to love each other here'

she

counting the joys and the sorrows
on the shell of a coccinellidae
and he
with the weight of two buttercups
in the palm of a hand
realising
this is an example of perfection
a beautiful place to die.

JAY WATSON

Bacchanalia

Quinaquina coca tree
Belladonna serenise
Ambuscado alchemy
Rioting in bawdy night.
Hops and barley, fruit of vine
Slyly spiced with papaver
Weaves a spell most hazardous
As the prudent watch takes flight.
When the torpid night turns pale
Innocence shed like serpent scales
Spew from the maws of shady lairs
Cannonade dishonoured light.
Fill the coffers clinch the deals
Intoxicated with success
Moloch will accept the corpses
Bacchus simply mocks their plight.

RICHARD UNWIN

Mill Yard

Cobbled together, grinding its teeth,
Hoping to gain yet one more life
Before it is done.
Stark with the wet of rain,
And dying by the developer's hand,
Graved by generations of clogs
That have tapped data into it
In record of futile human passage.
It lies with a written purpose:
To seed its secret knowledge.
Sick grasses grow around and in the gaps between
Reluctant to cover the worn stones
And become rooted in despond,
Which is some sort of revenge
For the unremitting toil it represents.
Still, it lies as a black curse,
For the potential of life was forbidden
To the damned that once had to walk there.

ALMIRA HOLMES

It Had a Picture of Sheep, and Was Older Than Me

The jigsaw was a sacred object
its 450 pieces not to be touched
by our profane hands. Only
She knew where all the pieces
should go. We must learn
on easier puzzles with pieces
designed with the novice
puzzler in mind.

Last year she came to visit
bearing the puzzle, giving
me three days to understand
its mysteries and with no-one
allowed to disturb me. Then
it was gone, back to its shrine.

MARTIN ZARROP

Satnav

He loves her voice,
the honeyed tones of one who knows
her stuff. She's in control.
She's made her choice

no sulks or headaches. Now
she does not speak.
Vindictive cow!
This is the second time this week

she's misbehaved. Enough
of this abuse of trust!
He reaches for the switch

then stops. The bitch
must know he dare not kill her off
and, in the silence, knows that he is lost.

The Finished Sentence of Love

'A love like ours…' you said,
failing to finish the sentence.

Finish the sentence!
Don't leave it hanging,
like a bird without wings,
or its truth will never be aired.

A love like ours is too big for me
to evoke poetically
using the usual symbols.

The moon, the stars,
the reddest Lancashire rose,
are all dear to my heart
but in no way can they do
justice to you.

Darling, I can't wait for any seas
to gang dry. I must speak my love now.
It goes beyond your skin,
your sweet temples
your aquamarine eyes,
and the amazing smell of you.
I love every day of your suffering life;
all that gave you your humanity.

My Love, with you in my life
the brickbats that abound
are of no consequence.
You give me the confidence
to finish every sentence;

to discern my conscience;
to be a prophet without honour
in his own land.

Though the poetic lexicon is inadequate
for expressions of a love like ours,
I have nearly finished the sentence.

But I must leave the end open.
A full stop would be wrong
for a love like ours

SHIRLEY NICHOLSON

From the Window

volcanic ash sunset

By bleached magnolia
moorhen paddle
sunset waters,
their tight-beaked eek
cuts across
a distance of peace.
Through the transparency
of budding willow,
rowan, alder, ash
the sun beckons.
Boughs are alight
with fairy light and,
caught in the calm,
I walk through the glass
on a footpath of air
and follow to the west.

Head Full of Paris

I do not ever want the incapacities and irritations of old age;
the endless loud voices
and over-enunciated words,
the earnestness in the eyes of the do-gooder
or the barely-veiled patronisation of the over-worked nurse,
compassion sterilised.

I do not ever want to fear ice,
or steep stairs,
or slipping in the bath.
I want my bones to always be this strong and supportive,
not brittle, temperamental, and inconsistent,
all too ready to abandon duty,
a faithful partner suddenly turned faithless.

I want my body that has always brought pleasure and
        vitality,
to keep on doing just this.
Not turn on me,
a family dog gone rabid,
forgetting the glorious friendship we once shared.

I do not fear death.
May death take me long before I forget
the names of my grandchildren,
or the street where I live;
or worse.
If I forget all that I am,
or ever was.
Let only death dress me in oblivion.

Let me always be like this.
Vibrant,
mischievous,
head full of Paris.
Salivating for words, ideas, colours, books, music.
Let it always be like this.
Then let it be gone.

The Real Icarus

The men have taken to shore,
drunk and singing, arm in arm with whores.
My son, their Captain, he yells, keep her fast,
sing my shanties or feel the lash.
Away away-oh, away away-oh.

Down by the docks he pisses on tramps,
shows them wax burns, all born from lamps.
In alleys, in taverns, he spreads his lies,
shows them goose feathers, bullshit flies.
Away away-oh, away away-oh.

I am immortal, says my son, women snigger,
cocks his pistol, smiles, pulls the trigger.
A snap, a fizz against wax, a misfired dud,
my son is not born of my blood.
Away away-oh, away away-oh.

Icarus fell here, women say, as I come and go,
in a tavern, in a marketplace, he performed his show.
No fizz, I melted the wax from the barrel of his gun,
he took away my home, my life, my inventions, my son.
Away away-oh, away away-oh.

CYNTHIA BUELL THOMAS

Lines on Picasso's *The Aperitif*

slim flower head
red pollen bold
erect on scarlet stalk
whispering scented smoke
with green breath absinthe moist
wormwood curled

the perfumed whiff of rosy cunt
pressed at bay
damp
between satin thighs
more sleek than silken stockings garter strapped
tantalizing roads to mossy fields
ungated

arm like a swan's neck
imperious
conducting conversations
her way
pulling and pushing the lusts of men
and women
with her acrobatic words
grinding mince
out of reasoned philosophies

she balances the tray surely
the phallic bottle and the open-lipped glass
upon her palm spread
braced against one sturdy ham
crossed over

Baptism

Rosary hails monthly grace
Maria, rinse your dress in salt
Your Christ is with you
On his knees
Wonderworking as you pray

Dispels the curse with gentle words
'Maria, rinse your dress in salt
Stigmata should not
Stain or taint
Nor pain come from the sword'

She lets the love of Jesus in
His trinity of rebels
Fingertips and tongue and lips
Release the blood of prophets

Ascending now with prayers out loud
The rapture washes over her
Rosé flows where roses grow
To splash upon the altar

Purifying robe of sin
Maria rinsed her dress in salt
Where Jesus' holy
Blood was spilt
Magnificat baptism

Melting Crayons

I reinvent the colour wheel but confuse the hue.
Never mind, my palette tends to blur the lines
As a metronome proffers a pattern for my seesaw state of
      mind,
I choose not to be frightened.
Instead inspired, flashgun fast.
But the contrary light that guides blinds.

So I saunter axis x and y and scale the contours of the folded.
But follow, and therefore arrive where others have
      outmoded.

Suddenly with a flick of the wrist my mind meanders to what
      can only be described as mauve.

DAVID HULME

Irene and Bert Rearrange the Furniture:
A Mantovani Interlude

Workers' Playtime
Bread and jam
Mantovani
Radiogram
Pause to wonder
Who I am.

I'm the boy who listens
To Irene and Bert
Rearranging the furniture,
Especially to Bert
Rearranging my Mam.

Mantovani,
Full and round
Far too soft
To drown the sound
Of breaking things
As Bert and Irene
Stiff-arm dance
To Mantovani's
Luscious strings.

Workers' Playtime
Bread and jam
Mantovani
Bam bam bam.

Then the silence
Radio hissing

Me asleep now
Gently pissing
On my dreams
Again.

Lucy Burns

Weekend Away

Campus crawling – I take the train home, cut
ties with old friends by keeping my visit
unannounced. Recovery days spent
drunk, snatching flies on Walcott beach, turning
the car round half-way to Norwich to see
straight across the water to Cantley, steam
still rising from the sugar-beet factory.
Midnight on UEA campus, walking
up to this flat in the Ziggurat slopes,
when at once, my vision folds out like a
dressing-table mirror and I'm back on
Brighton breakwater, splitting drinks with friends.
They talk about yesterday's house-party,
I watch Jonny's top lip roll-up above
his front teeth. His snaggle-tooth has capsized,
upending his smile in a slant. Later
when rumours turn to slur I hear Norwich
at my back, sending me up the overpass
to empty graduate student houses.
The city walls lean, and mid-step I'm back
to front, trying to remember the last
time I came to visit. Each trip they seem
thinner, confused about where I've been, who
spoke last. A shaded rash on the side of
Iain's face curls up around his eye like
a question mark, and I take the train back.

Richard Hughes

Terminus and a Dream of Rewinding

Did someone warn that certain cities
are best not entered for the first time
in early December after evening rain?
Well this is one of them. And here you are.

The yellow coach draws up at a makeshift
terminus, a sloping yard in the approach
to a disused railway station.

A huge clock, in a dream of rewindings,
moons over wrought iron lattice work.
One day, inside the vault, you'll see empty
platforms stretch nowhere like fingers in rigor.

Above it all those busy starlings
settle to roost on gable and portico,
premature revenants of the life
you left behind. Hundreds of them,
an urban wonder. One day they'll have to go.

Wearing bright new thoughts of beginnings,
you step down, head up, hope folded crisply
and tucked under your arm. But the thrill of toeing
the edge of a future filters your senses.

Now, twenty years on, in recollection,
when you breathe that night's air – thick, as if rife
with smut from doused bonfires of old tyres –
looming memorial halls menace
corners, warehouses block the ends of streets;
dampness clads the walls of Victorian facades.

And twenty years on, still in the act
of stepping down, you change your mind,
retake your seat to plan for tomorrow
a morning climb on foot to apple picking
through mist whose Cotswold wash renews
the yellow coaches on their journeys home.

Tourist Information

the North Face
of the Largest Peardrop In T' World

has still not been conquered
Just outside the Town Hall

is the spot where Early Man said
'eh up, there's trouble at 'mill'

mum asleep on the sofa

the food that clothed the Empire was Hot Pot

you can visit six days, take home
handy hints and
Coltsfoot Rock   Chocolate Limes

I visit once a week

which reminds me   concerning the myth
of the shotgun shack   read

our explanatory pamphlet details
iron age burial mounds &

the largest collection of Tiffany glass
outside America

that's the home

where she lives   when everything stopped
dragging fists invented industrialisation

they look after her
she gets confused

Elvis went to our grammar school,
    discovered rock'n'roll

he did

doesn't know where she is

Potatoes   Neck end of lamb   Carrots

    now she says she never liked lamb

in the woodwork room where Hendrix
built his first guitar

didn't he

I made a memory box
then forgot where I put it

Manchester Poem

The sun and I are glancing off
your high walls to heaven:
your dear glazed bricks, your
fast iron, cast-iron studs,
your gushing locks.

Monumentally,
you soared in 1895
with a mind for Arts and Crafts,
Ars Laboris. Kept on soaring.
Rose from the Irwell
who still murmurs darkly.

We see her over the plated,
riveted bridges,
a creature disturbed,
disturbing;
still glimpse the private lady,
industrial, black,
bemused, below,
between Joshua Brooks and
The Lass O'Blairgowrie.

Factories of the mental kind,
glass and chrome,
Avatar-coloured
are clambering up these days.
Now it's MMU
monumentally soaring
with hard-faced,
glass-faced
commerce.

MATTHEW JUDGE

The Hot Blood of Youth

First cold of the first, then, little cold,
then ghost sent assured with cold heaven held.
The middle upon finding itself, finds itself neat-ripped,
a tear between two frays, and a survey of lip.
And the seamstress at the end of the quality-control line,
sports, as she walks out beneath grey summer sky,
the quiet burden that the grey clouds shoulder too,
striding storm held in place, and only minutes after noon.

LINDA SUNDERLAND

Dream Couples

I dreamt that Charles Bukowski and Marianne Moore
got laid.
They'd met in a downtown bar
and he'd liked the way she fastened the buttons
on her crêpe de Chine blouse
all the way up to the neck.

They went back to his place and fell into bed
after finishing the Jack Daniels.
She kissed very nicely,
but her tongue was steel.
Later he threw up in her fedora.

Next morning when he woke, she was up already.
'*My father used to say,*' she said, fastening her stockings
and straightening the seams,
'*Superior people never make long visits.*'
'*Your father's an asshole,*' he said.

Over breakfast I asked Tom what he thought.
'*I should have been a pair of ragged claws
scuttling across the floor of silent seas*,' he said,
buttering the last of the crumpets
and turning to the poetry reviews in the TLS.

'*All your beauty, all your wit, is a gift, my dear,
from me*,' I said.

Elaine Booth

Negative Capability

I want to reverberate in your mind:
I want you to remember this grim night,
first and last by kindnesses and killings.
The fabric of existence will buckle
at the strain, and fade in a fold of time.
I want all ends to be met by all means,
all tides safe shepherded home by the moon,
where no darkness sleeps to no awakening.
The struggle to meaning finds hands empty,
too cold to shiver their way back to life.
Set your star to the other direction,
no magnetic point of compass detects
word-ghosts, in love, as Echo, with themselves:
meaning transcending to a wordless song.

Ron Priestner

Dearth

Inside that stony, cold, old place,
There, once, I felt an ember glow,
And held within its warmth your face
Inside that stony, cold, old place.
There, still, your touch, your kisses trace
A frozen pattern in the snow
Inside that stony, cold, old place,
Where, once, I felt an ember glow.

Natalie Clarke

Life Aim

I wish I was in love;
Then I could be smug,
And not give a shit.

EDYTH WARD

Weekend Away

The top drawer in the dressing table
smells of someone else's perfume.
Someone else's cigarette
has put a mark on the dressing table top.
The beds are hard but for two days
we belonged to this room.
The fluffy whites droop in the bathroom,
the hotel soap sits in its own juices
and the shower caps have eloped.
In the wardrobe the non-steal coat hangers
clink together waiting to do battle
with the next resident's clothes.
There's always a broken one,
who leans against the others
in the empty wardrobe.

Someone had messed up
the digital alarm clock in the room
and it wakened us at one in the morning.
We couldn't find the "off" button
and the noise awoke the room next door,
who banged on the wall.
We think it was the man with the wig
and the woman who doesn't have
the cooked breakfast, who sit on table six.

The room is stripped of us.
Dirty glasses group together,
the bin is full of yesterday's papers,
tissues and an old pair of natural tan tights.
The comfort tray has been drained
of all but the sugar.

Tomorrow he will make tea and coffee
for someone else.
There's a tug on the heart when we leave,
as the "Do not disturb" notice on the door
rocks a gentle goodbye.

Paul J Burgess

Beside

I see you now, not all that you once were, at least no longer
to the physical eye, but intact, still.
I wonder this and that, and that and this, whether my right
to wonder or not, I do.
Maybe a poem would break the spell, or shell, the film the
field the barrier, behind which, beyond which, through
which, you reside intact.
I still believe.
Whether it is my right to believe or not, I do.
I can remain here, where I have been now for some time,
and wait.
Though it is not a place, or time, simply a state.
You may need a hand to take the leap.
I dare not push too much, but I still have to push, some.
Whether it is my right to push or not, I do.
Not hoping or wanting or waiting for a crack, unless it is one
made with your own conscious and decisive and realistic
thoughts.
That crack I would be happy to see, but would not want to
suggest or impress or invite.
At least, not from me, or for me, or in any way because of
me.
And maybe you are happy in there, and maybe one day I
will realise this and the state will end and the wait will end
and a different path will be walked.
Still near, or aside, and when needed behind. Just, in some
ways, different.
I am after all. A friend.

SUE BARNARD

Clerihew's Lament

Edmund Clerihew Bentley
wrote "Trent's Last Case" very intently.
But his main claim to fame
was the biographical verse-form which bears his name.

Four lines. First, the subject's name. One of the verse-form's
        strengths
is that the four lines, whatever else they might contain, can
        be of wildly differing lengths.
But the rhyme scheme must always be
AABB.

I am sure there are many who
have tried to write a Clerihew
but have then got stuck
for a final rhyme.

Facebook Friends

Friends, family, Facebookers, status update;
It's ev'ry hour, on the hour, round the clock.
It's what I'm eating, what I think about,
Or see myself tagged in your photograph.
Now Freddy Frogspawn sends a friend request
But I don't recognise his photograph.
It doesn't help that it's a plastic duck.
But Facebook says we seem acquainted;
And Facebook is an honourable site.
Perhaps tomorrow I may yet friend him.
Now I go looking for an old school friend;
Her name is Pasadena Battersby.
A search reveals one hundred of that name.
A better bet Friends Reunited is,
But I am Facebook-faithful, all the same;
And Facebook says we seem acquainted;
And Facebook is an honourable site.
I send a Friend Request to ev'ry one.
My daughter's on-line boyfriend sends a quiz
To see how sane I am. I hardly dare
To tick the boxes. I'm a psychopath!
I've long suspected, but who is this guy?
I've never really met him; nor has she;
But Facebook says we seem acquainted;
And Facebook is an honourable site.
I wonder if he's got a friend for me.
The chocolate breakfast cereal that I Krave,
And Pampers nappies, and the Lloyd's Hotel,
And countless more need me, on commerce bent,
To join their Facebook following.
Yes, Facebook says we seem acquainted;

And Facebook is an honourable site.
You never know, they may give gifts away.
A picture on the topmost right appears
Of someone Facebook says that I may know.
We have in common friends galore, it seems;
At last count it was fourteen hundred, but
Despite the fact he seems to live next door
I cannot say I heard his name before.
Yet Facebook says we seem acquainted;
And Facebook is an honourable site.
A chat on-line seems safer than the street.
'Facebook is friends, friends Facebook,' – that is all
Ye know on earth, and all ye need to know.

HUGH POLEHAMPTON

Chance Encounter

Bonjour! Bonjour! So smooth, so mellifluous,
softly spoken words, but carrying such powerful meaning
of welcome, of respect, such a caring greeting.
From behind me on the boat your voice turned me like a
    magnet.
Our eyes met.
Wow! Electrical discharge of instant appreciation.
You appeared relaxed, confident, well dressed,
a carefully tended moustache
perfectly shaped to your upper lip and cheeks,
setting off well your angular cheekbones.
You had a classic beauty,
just one small sign of hidden agitation
that showed the faintest hint
of the volcano hidden beneath this apparent order,
perhaps created by some hideous violent events long gone.
It was your hair.
Curling lavishly over your neck it had a wild quality
that said it will not be controlled or shaped by convention.
It had a quirkiness that enticed me
but also made me wary.
We talked.
I could listen to your rhythmic flirtatious romantic voice for
    ever, not bothering about any meaning.
But forcing myself to listen to your thoughts,
they were logical, and carefully but passionately presented.
As I got to know you better, I continued to be wary.
That volcano could flare up and shower me with rocks and
    fire,
I loved it, it kept me on my toes
to treat you respectfully and when I misjudged things
to learn to fire back, to duel with you.
Normally we both survived.

ROBIN GRAHAM

Elm Street Engine
(Museum of Science and Industry)

Note! When you listen carefully, the engine makes four
          sounds:
Tug-tug here…
H-hmmm…
Oh brother, oh-dear mother,
Clip-clop…
These are a poem in themselves!

'Let me be free!' is the flywheel's lament
Of the never weary-limbed old mill engine.
'No giddy mouse could keep running with me,
I'd power through girders if I could run free,
Now you power me up for the public to see,
Oh brother, oh-dear mother, oh brother, oh-dear mother.'

Endless revolving and churning and hissing
And click hollow clanging, head throbbing, enduring,
Relentlessly up and down pistons keep driving
As cogs keep engaging with flywheel flying
And steam threads fade quickly disappear to nothing,
'Tug-tug here, h-hmmm, tug-tug here, h-hmmm.'

Alive is the flywheel with arms and hip wiggle
And panels with bolts that look like silver faces,
The pressure gauge eyes are forever surveying,
Hot oil and water body odour fine spraying,
Pistons with oil smears like a face that needs wiping
'Clip-clop, clip-clop.'

I stop off the steam and the flywheel slows down
I operate wheels like a captain of industry

I open a valve and I hear life escape.
Wafts of moist oil-filled air comes to greet me.
The gentle giant becomes still.

'Ladies and gentlemen, the museum closes in ten minutes.'
We leave the Elm Street Mill Engine
To its memories,
History,
Glory.

MIKE PEACE

College Canteen

Bright yellow chairs surround
plastic blue tables,
trodden chips drown in spilt drinks,
crumbs on table tops, sandwich boxes
and vacuumed hot coffee pots.
Cigarette dimp-filled ashtrays,
hot tea rings and dirty plates.
Stainless steel salt and pepper pots
reflect the faces of the canteen ladies
as they wipe the smiles off each other's
tables.

P TRYTHALL

The Iron Men

Stare out
    from the shore
        from the shore
            to the sea
                to the sea
                    from the shore
                and they stand
            in the sea
      and they stand
    on the shore
in the stones
    in the slime
in the sand

and they stare
    and they stare
blind eyed

to the sea

and are
silent.

Lightning Source UK Ltd.
Milton Keynes UK
UKOW050913020112

184604UK00001B/1/P